★★★ THE ★★★ FREEDOM AGENDA

★★★ THE ★★★
FREEDOM
AGENDA

Why a Balanced Budget Amendment
Is Necessary to Restore
Constitutional Government

SENATOR MIKE LEE

Since 1947
REGNERY
PUBLISHING, INC.
An Eagle Publishing Company • Washington, DC

Cataloging-in-Publication data on file with the Library of Congress
ISBN 978-1-59698-288-8

Published in the United States by
Regnery Publishing, Inc.
One Massachusetts Avenue, NW
Washington, DC 20001
www.regnery.com
Manufactured in the United States of America

10 9 8 7 6 5 4 3 2 1
Books are available in quantity for promotional or premium use. For information on discounts or terms, write to Director of Special Sales, Regnery Publishing, Inc., One Massachusetts Avenue NW, Washington, DC 20001, or call (202) 216-0600.

Distributed to the trade by:
Perseus Distribution
387 Park Avenue South
New York, NY 10016

To my children, James, John, and Eliza.

Contents

PART IV
FOUR ESSENTIAL DOCUMENTS

Introduction

Every day, America comes one step closer to fiscal insolvency. Federal spending has skyrocketed from roughly 2 percent of GDP a hundred years ago to over 25 percent in 2011—a staggering 1,500 percent increase in spending as a percentage of GDP. Our national debt now stands at more than $14 trillion— roughly $50,000 for every man, woman, and child in America. And we are adding around $1.65 trillion to that debt every year—about $5,500 per living American. Stated differently, for every family of four, the federal government has already incurred $200,000 in debt and is adding new debt of roughly $22,000 per year.

At this rate, we could more than double our debt by 2020. Our annual interest payments alone could then reach nearly a trillion dollars—more than we currently spend on national defense, Social Security, or Medicare and Medicaid combined. Meanwhile, our entitlement liabilities will be expanding so fast that mandatory spending—defined as entitlement spending and interest on national debt combined—will likely match or exceed our *entire annual budget*.

Our economy cannot survive this ruinous level of debt. But the federal government is incapable of pulling us back from the brink of fiscal Armageddon. In its spending mania, it has run roughshod over the careful constitutional checks and balances our Founders designed to prevent the emergence of the exact kind of overly powerful, spendthrift government we have today. A government that is too powerful and has access to too much money simply can't be relied upon to self-correct.

Politicians recognize the problem but are incapable of fixing it. For example, President Obama spoke boldly of the need for spending restraint in his 2011 State of the Union Address to Congress. "Every day, families sacrifice to live within their means," he declared. "They deserve a government that does the same."[1] However, in the very same speech Obama undermined this message by advocating a host of new federal spending measures—using the euphemism "investments"—to speed up our economic recovery.

This was the same argument the president used to justify his exorbitant, $800 billion "stimulus" program. Although that spending binge failed to improve the economy, with unemployment rising from 7.6 percent when the stimulus passed to roughly

9 percent today, it looks like Obama's prescription is more of the same. A few weeks after his State of the Union speech, the president proposed a budget with yet another record deficit—one exceeding $1.65 trillion. Unsurprisingly, as I write these words, the federal government hit its debt ceiling, sparking demands from the Obama administration to raise the ceiling even higher.

Congress has proven no more responsible than President Obama. For decades, members of Congress have resorted to perpetual deficit spending to keep and expand all the government programs demanded by their influential supporters and other special interests.

Due to all this unsustainable spending, eventually the federal government will be forced to either increase taxes or inflate the currency to stave off fiscal insolvency. Either of those moves, which are only short-term fixes anyway, will severely degrade the liberty and prosperity of the taxpayers.

Even if Congress and the president somehow agreed on a balanced budget, it would undoubtedly prove to be another short-term fix—history shows there is nothing more impermanent than a balanced budget. For example, look at New Jersey. After taking office in 2010, Governor Chris Christie erased an estimated $11 billion budget deficit almost entirely through spending cuts. Thanks to Christie's policies, by May 2011 New Jersey's economy was turning around, and the state treasurer projected the Garden State would rake in half a billion dollars in extra tax revenue.

And what was the reaction of the Democrat-controlled New Jersey legislature? Did its members hail Christie for his fiscal rectitude? Of course not. In fact, they cited the unexpected tax windfall as proof that the state *didn't need* austerity. "The governor has balanced his budgets on the backs of the middle class, now this gives us an opportunity to undo that," said State Senator Paul Sarlo. Assembly budget committee chairman Lou Greenwald, seemingly rendered incoherent by his dismay at a balanced budget, insisted the extra tax money should be used to "restore [sic] some of the pain" caused by Christie's spending cuts. Eventually, the decision on how to use the extra tax revenue was largely taken out of Christie's hands; the New Jersey Supreme Court, apparently agreeing there was no need for austerity, ordered Christie to increase education funding by $500 million—the same amount as the estimated tax windfall.[2]

The trend is the same on the federal level—Congress balanced the budget in the late 1990s, but look where we are now. Far from permanently enshrining responsible spending policies, a balanced budget more often ushers in a new spending spree, as politicians feel absolutely obligated to spend themselves back into deficits.

With our government incapable of staving off our looming fiscal doomsday, we have reached the point where we need to adopt a far-reaching, structural reform that will provide not a short-term fix, but a long-term solution to the kind of reckless over-spending and expansion of federal power that now threaten our republic. While statutory reforms will prove both helpful and necessary, we need something stronger—a permanent mechanism that restricts Congress's spending authority.

★ ★ ★

This book argues that a balanced budget amendment is the solution for extricating America from our fiscal crisis and for limiting the size and scope of government. Conservatives sometimes argue that passing such an amendment, though desirable, is politically impossible. I used to think so myself, and in fact, I thought the entire idea of emphasizing constitutional issues to be a losing political platform—until I got elected to the U.S. Senate on just such a platform.

Here's how my campaign unfolded: in early 2009, I found myself wondering what would become of the Republican Party and of the conservative cause in general. America had just elected a liberal Democrat to the White House and had increased the Democrats' majorities in both houses of Congress. The Democrats' agenda was clear: more government spending, bigger and more intrusive government, socialized medicine, rising deficits, and a ballooning national debt.

Like many Republicans, I blamed my own party for much of this disaster. Our national debt had increased more during the twelve-year period in which the GOP controlled Congress (including a six-year stretch in which Republicans also controlled the White House) than it had in any comparable period in history. Despite their small-government rhetoric, congressional Republicans during that time had expanded the size, reach, and cost of the federal government and had even nudged America toward nationalized healthcare, often breaching the constitutional limits on their authority in the process. With this sorry record, Republicans got crushed at the polls in 2008 because they failed to provide a real alternative to the Democratic agenda.

In February 2009, I was explaining my frustrations to my friend Monte Bateman, a Utah conservative activist. I told him that the antidote to the perpetual expansion and "mission creep" of the federal government is found in the enumerated-powers doctrine—that is, the notion that the Constitution gives the federal government only limited, enumerated powers, while reserving all other powers to the states. This doctrine, I argued, could serve as the basis for a new, limited-government political movement—one focusing on the Constitution's bedrock, party-neutral principles of federalism.

Still, I told Monte that I doubted any candidate could get elected on such a platform. I thought voters would be bored by talk about things like Article I, Section 8 (the part of the Constitution that lists nearly every power possessed by Congress), the Tenth Amendment (explaining that powers not granted to Congress in the Constitution are reserved to the states), textualism (a strict, literal reading of the Constitution), and originalism (a reading that focuses on the founding generation's understanding of each word and phrase at the time it was added to the Constitution).

I was familiar with these topics because my father—the late Rex E. Lee, a professor of Constitutional Law who served as the U.S. Solicitor General during the Reagan administration—talked about them with me, my brother, and my five sisters around the dinner table. I may have been thirty before I realized that not every family discusses the Constitution's Presentment Clause over mashed potatoes. But I eventually learned through trial and error (mostly error) that people rarely find that document as interesting as I do.

After wondering aloud whether my political ideas could resonate with anyone besides lawyers, Monte asked if I would give a speech to some of his friends summarizing my approach. I agreed, and on February 19, 2009, I spoke to a few dozen people at Monte's house. My speech focused on the text and history of the Constitution, and on the founding generation's abiding concern that large, national governments tend to become tyrannical unless their power is carefully checked. Local governments, by contrast, tend to operate closer to the people and show more accountability, but they are unable to perform certain national tasks such as providing for national defense. Consequently, I explained, the Founding Fathers went to great lengths to ensure that, while Congress would possess every power necessary to ensure our survival as a nation, all other powers— meaning *most* powers wielded by government—would remain with the states.

I argued that our government was based on this concept of limited, enumerated powers for nearly 150 years before the structure began to deteriorate during the New Deal era, especially after the Supreme Court adopted an extraordinarily broad interpretation of the Commerce Clause—one that, taken to its logical extreme, would authorize Congress to regulate every aspect of human existence.

I noted that the Supreme Court was never intended to be the sole, exclusive guardian of the Constitution, in the sense that officials serving in all three branches of government are required to take an oath to uphold it. That requirement, in my view, compels members of Congress to exercise self-restraint in recognition of their limited, enumerated powers. In other words, Congress is not necessarily complying with the letter or spirit of the Constitution just because the Supreme Court has generally allowed it to expand its own powers.

At some point during the last several decades, I concluded, Congress stopped asking whether it *could* exercise almost any power imaginable. Why? Because, with only two exceptions over the last seventy-five years, the Supreme Court's answer has always been "yes." And when Congress stopped asking the question whether it *could* expand its power, it also stopped asking whether it *should*. Thus, our federal government has grown exponentially since the New Deal, and with it our taxes, our enormous regulatory burden, and our national debt.

The solution, I proposed, is for the American people to demand that whenever any member of Congress votes to fund a federal program or create a new one, that person should explain where Congress gets its constitutional authority to run that program. Those who can't supply satisfactory answers should be voted out of office and replaced by candidates who believe the Constitution actually means what it says. As more adherents of the enumerated powers doctrine get elected and those who oppose it lose their seats, Congress will begin to restore meaningful limits on federal power. And as the states regain their lost sovereignty, we will see a dramatic reduction in everything from massive deficit spending to punitive and confiscatory taxation to oppressive regulation.

I was stunned by the reaction to my speech. I had been afraid I would put my audience to sleep, but instead they enthusiastically applauded my remarks, with several people offering to help if I decided to run for federal office. One such person was Connie Smith, a soldier's wife and grandmother who offered to set up a series of speaking events for me around Utah. She made an argument that I found utterly irrefutable: "Regardless of whether you decide to run for office, you will be spreading a message that people need to hear and initiating a statewide, grassroots-level discussion that needs to happen."

Over the next few months, I spoke all over the state—in Salt Lake City, Ogden, Provo, Logan, Vernal, St. George, and countless places in between—and on each occasion my listeners reacted as favorably as those in Monte's home. Addressing growing audiences in public libraries, high school gymnasiums, and private residences, I was shocked that so many people in so many communities would show up on a perfectly good Thursday, Friday, or Saturday night just to hear someone talk about the Constitution.

At the end of each event, people approached me and asked how they could get involved in promoting the ideas I was championing. By late summer, my speaking events had developed something of an independent following. State legislators and other civic leaders across Utah began offering to organize, publicize, and host my speeches in their own communities. Although the mainstream news media rarely covered my speeches, they drew the attention of bloggers and other elements of the "new media."

As our nascent, limited-government movement gathered supporters and volunteers, we decided to form an organization to serve as the vehicle for the message of constitutionally limited government. We named the organization the "Article I Society," recognizing the part of the Constitution that outlines the basic powers that properly belong to the federal government. By November 2009, the Article I Society had signed up hundreds of volunteers from nearly every part of the state. Most of the

Society's volunteers, I suspect, were tea partiers who already saw that the 2010 election could be a watershed event in American history.

Finally, on January 5, 2010, I announced my candidacy for the U.S. Senate. Throughout my campaign, my ideas drew an enthusiastic response from everyday people who understood that our federal government, having shaken off all constitutional restraint, has amassed an unsustainable debt that threatens every man, woman, and child in this country. My message resonated far more thoroughly and effectively than I ever imagined it would. It proved what so many had doubted: that a platform focused on constitutionally limited government can win.

★ ★ ★

Crucially, during my campaign I frequently championed a balanced budget amendment. It seemed many voters hadn't given the issue much thought, so I explained why this single reform is the linchpin both for restoring constitutional limits on federal power and for resolving our fiscal crisis. Once the issue was framed in this way, I found my listeners overwhelmingly supported the idea.

I quickly concluded that a balanced budget amendment is indeed possible, and that the biggest obstacle to adopting it is the simple *perception* that it can't be done. In order to begin changing that perception, I decided the American people could use a clear, concise argument for why a balanced budget amendment is so important, how it can help restore constitutionally limited government, and how it can get adopted. And that's what this book sets out to explain.

Part I of *The Freedom Agenda* outlines the enumerated powers doctrine—the notion that the Constitution created a federal government authorized to wield only limited, "enumerated" powers. It also details why the Founding Fathers were so committed to constitutionally limited government, how we have drifted from it, and the preliminary steps we can take to restore it.

Part II argues that the only reliable way to permanently balance the budget is by adopting a balanced budget amendment, and it explains how balancing the budget will help to restore constitutionally limited government.

Part III describes how, just as efforts to balance the budget will help to restore constitutionally limited government, so too will efforts to restore constitutionally limited government help us to balance the budget.

Part IV provides some crucial documents that readers will find useful in our struggle to restore limited government, as envisioned by America's Founders.

Whether you are most concerned about improving our economy, shoring up our national defense, or preserving entitlements like Social Security, Medicare, and Medicaid, you should support a balanced budget amendment. After all, our economy, national defense, and entitlements are all jeopardized by our crushing national debt.

For this reason, the debt crisis is neither a conservative nor a liberal issue. It is neither Republican nor Democratic. It is, simply, an American issue.

Saddling our children and grandchildren with this debt is unconscionable. But it would be foolish to think our overspending will only affect future generations. This is an existential crisis that, if left unresolved, will dramatically impact our lives in the near future. We can still fix the problem, but the clock is ticking. The time to act is now—for our children's sake as well as our own.

PART I

★ ★ ★

The Case for Constitutionally Limited Government

CHAPTER ONE

★ ★ ★

Liberty and Government Action: A Zero-Sum Game

L ike good neighbors, good governments know and respect boundaries. Similarly, bad governments—like bad neighbors—fail to recognize any meaningful difference between their own business and the business of others. But unlike bad neighbors, bad governments have certain tools that, if abused, can destroy not just the tranquility of a neighborhood, but the freedom, prosperity, and survival of an entire nation. Governments should therefore be subject to defined boundaries that—like fences that define the boundaries between two neighboring landowners—mark the limits of their power.

America's Founding Fathers understood this principle, having suffered the abuses of a London-based government that had access to vast, seemingly limitless resources and recognized no real limits on its power. Accordingly, the Founders carefully crafted the fundamental document of our republic, the U.S. Constitution, to limit the role of the federal government to a few limited or "enumerated" powers needed to fulfill national responsibilities. These powers included regulating commerce between the states and with foreign nations; establishing an army and a navy and otherwise providing for national defense; declaring war; establishing a uniform system of weights and measures; and protecting intellectual property. Crucially, the Founders specified that powers not granted to the federal government would be reserved to the states.

We have drifted far from that understanding in recent decades, largely because the Supreme Court rarely enforces limits on Congress's authority. Congress has interpreted the Court's inaction as a constitutional green light for constantly expanding its own power. Thus, members of Congress routinely assume that any and every problem can—and should—be addressed at the national level, regardless of any constitutional restraints. When members of Congress are occasionally forced to cite their authority for adopting some measure, they typically cite Supreme Court precedents that imply Congress is empowered to regulate nearly every aspect of human existence.

Today, the fight for a balanced budget amendment is part of a larger battle to restore constitutionally limited government—a system in which, as James Madison explained in Federalist No. 45, the powers of the federal government are "few and defined," while those reserved to the states are "numerous and indefinite." This governing structure is rooted in the ancient, unassailable notion that liberty is preferable to tyranny. The founding generation understood that the former is more likely to exist—and to give rise to its principal byproduct, prosperity—where the power of government is limited. It is up to our generation to restore the Founders' vision.

★ ★ ★

To understand why the founding generation insisted so adamantly on constitutionally limited government, we must first understand the delicate relationship between liberty and government action.

Liberty is the ability of each individual to live, act, and enjoy his own property without external coercion, interference, or control; in other words, it is the capacity to live and act affirmatively rather than being acted upon. Liberty is a gift from God. It exists without any earthly sovereign bestowing it upon us, and will remain with us unless or until an external, coercive force takes it away by, for example, threatening our lives or degrading our property rights.

The purpose of government is to *constrain* human behavior through coercion. Therefore, when government acts, it does so at the expense of individual liberty. In fact, government action and individual liberty can fairly be described as competitors in a zero-sum game—to whatever degree a government acts, individual liberty is diminished to that extent.

That doesn't mean *all* government action is bad; in many instances we need the government to act to protect a person's life, liberty, or property against potential threats from others.

Without government we would live in anarchy—an awful condition in which the protection of life, liberty, and property would be left to each family or individual. In such a state, weaker individuals would be at the mercy of the aggressive and the strong.

Accordingly, there are instances when we must sacrifice a degree of individual liberty in order to authorize government action that, on balance, tends to enhance each individual's personal security and property interests.

While normally focused on protecting life, liberty, and property, government action may be warranted in some circumstances—primarily at the state and local level—where the government in question is tasked with establishing essential infrastructure that, while benefiting the public at large, probably would not exist without government involvement. Examples of such infrastructure include public roads, public schools, and public parks, all of which are normally administered at the state and local level.

Essential infrastructure aside, however, government action should normally be limited to the protection of life, liberty, and property. Every law and government action should be examined with those objectives in mind.

Consider laws against theft. Let's say I stole something from my friend Fred Roberts. Because of anti-theft laws, if I swiped something from Fred—especially something valuable like his diamond-studded pinkie ring—I would expect to:

1. Get arrested. (While charitable souls, Fred and his wife Penny are firm believers in the rule of law and would immediately call the police.)

2. Be prosecuted, convicted, and punished with a
   severe fine and/or prison sentence.

These consequences would dissuade me from stealing from
Fred. Anti-theft laws can therefore be said to restrict my liberty,
but I don't mind because, at least for me, foregoing theft is like
foregoing the right to eat dirt or shards of glass; it is far from a
sacrifice. I firmly believe in that old-fashioned, Judeo-Christian
tenet that stealing is wrong and is rightfully condemned by an
all-knowing, just God.

(To be fair, Fred owns no such ring, but I can easily imagine
him wearing one, and I would find a strange satisfaction in
mocking him for doing so. However, since Fred—a former
power forward for the Boston Celtics—is taller, stronger, and
faster than I am, and could probably beat me to a pulp with one
arm tied behind his back, I'll keep my mockery of him purely
hypothetical.)

Although anti-theft laws impinge on my liberty, I actually
benefit from them because they protect *my* property. They also
help to protect my life, which would be endangered without
those laws because I would have to personally defend my property against all intruders without the help of the police. In this
way, laws protecting private property also tend to protect life,
while they can be tailored to have a minimal impact on individual liberty.

For similar reasons, laws protecting life also tend to protect
property; if a person is safe from physical attack by others, his
property is more likely to be secure. And here again, a well-
written law protecting life—for example, a law prohibiting

murder—will have little or no effect on the liberty of freedom-loving people who rightfully attach significant value to each person's God-given right to live.

Overall, the most defensible laws are those that, while designed to protect either life or property, simultaneously protect both, with a minimal reduction of individual liberty. Laws criminalizing acts like theft, murder, kidnapping, and rape—activities that threaten the sanctity of life and property—easily satisfy this test.

★ ★ ★

We can't say the same of every law. In each instance, society must measure the benefits of government action against the corresponding erosion of individual liberty. In a free republic, elected officials should consider that tradeoff each time they approve government action, and citizens should hold them accountable whenever they err in applying this test.

Under this standard, the *least* defensible laws are those that, regardless of their stated objectives, excessively or unnecessarily undermine life, liberty, or property interests. A hypothetical example of such a law would be one imposing the death penalty on anyone who accidentally trespasses on someone else's property. Although that law might protect private property, it would needlessly jeopardize human life and individual liberty. Most people will be deterred from trespassing simply by the threat of fines or lawsuits, and in any event, given that trespassing is a common indiscretion that usually causes no lasting harm to person or property, no one could seriously contend that the death penalty would be a reasonable punishment.

Not every example is so clear-cut. What about laws that remove a child from the home of parents whom the government deems unfit? On one hand, such laws could prove necessary to protect a child's well-being. On the other hand, depending on how such laws are written, interpreted, and administered, they could severely undermine parents' liberty to raise their child in their own home and in the manner they deem appropriate.

What about tax laws? Taxes are necessary because they fund the operations of government. But the collection of taxes—even slight taxes—inherently impinges on taxpayers' property rights and undermines their individual liberty. Many taxpayers are required to spend *months* every year working, in effect, for the government. And when people pay taxes, they typically forfeit property and liberty that, once taken, will not and cannot be returned.

Thus, *any* law creating a government program that costs money—as essentially *all* government programs do—diminishes the liberty and property interests of taxpayers. Any time the taxpayer spends working for money that goes to the government is time the taxpayer can't spend with his family, reading books, reorganizing his sock drawer, or giving speeches about the Constitution.

My point here is simple: government spending *inevitably* interferes with liberty and property. Consequently, legislators at all levels of government should constantly ask themselves whether each expenditure they authorize can be justified in light of its impact on the liberty and property interests of taxpayers.

That question, if asked at all, is typically answered with the cavalier assertion that the expenditure accomplishes something good, somewhere, for someone. That isn't enough. Lawmakers should consider not just what the beneficiary gains, but what the taxpayer loses. Unless the expenditure's objective is something only the government can achieve—without excessively or unnecessarily impinging on individual liberty or property—lawmakers should reject the program.

Citizens shouldn't assume that innocuous and benevolent-sounding programs—for example, a government-sponsored midnight basketball league—have no impact on individual liberty. Such programs cost money; that money must be provided by taxpayers; and each time we raise taxes, we are extending the three, four, or five months that Americans spend every year working to earn money that the government will confiscate. Again, that precious time—whether it's minutes, hours, days, or weeks—is something we won't ever get back.

Proponents of new government programs lull us into submission by assuring us that (a) each taxpayer's share of *their* government program is minuscule, and (b) *their* government program will promote a worthy cause. This sophistry causes lawmakers and citizens alike to focus primarily on the putative benefits of a new program, and only secondarily, if at all, on the program's costs. And of course, politicians generally prefer playing the role of Santa Claus, who doles out government goodies, to the role of the Grinch, who says "no" to all these wonderful programs. Although few would deny that we need Grinches in government, not many politicians are willing to play that role.

The problem we face, to paraphrase economist Milton Friedman, is that government programs have concentrated benefits and dispersed costs. Those who benefit from a government program *really* want that program. Taxpayers may not want to pay for it, but they don't object because the cost of each new program is usually so widely dispersed that it is almost imperceptible. This problem is most acute at the federal level, where the costs of a new program are dispersed among the largest number of taxpayers.

But an expenditure is not justified merely because each taxpayer's loss may be less than each beneficiary's gain; that just means the program's true cost will be relatively easy to disguise. When we consider the aggregated cost of countless government programs, we see how the problem of concentrated benefits and dispersed costs can lead to a steady and dangerous, albeit subtle, erosion of liberty and property.

This is the primary reason why citizens of any free republic must clearly define and strictly limit the role of government. Such limits will protect the public from tyranny, but only to the extent that the limitations are both known and enforced by voters. This can happen only where voters insist on having the difficult, but necessary, discussion regarding the relative costs and benefits of each government program.

As noted above, we should have this discussion not only about taxes and spending, but about *every* new law or government program. But because we often don't, the government increasingly exercises its power arbitrarily, without restraint, to the detriment of individual liberty. This moves us in the direction of tyranny.

Having been born in a revolt against tyranny, America has made enormous sacrifices to spread freedom throughout the world. And when tyranny does arise, we aggressively destroy it before it destroys us. But unless we are vigilant toward our own government, tyranny will emerge by stealth and ensnare us by degrees before we even realize that our hard-fought liberties have been eroded beyond recognition.

★ ★ ★

CHAPTER TWO

The Rise and Fall of America's Constitutional Debate

Our Founding Fathers understood that every government becomes more susceptible to tyranny as it amasses more wealth and power. Any leader—whether a king, an elected president, or an elected president who thinks he's a king—can become a tyrant, and likely *will* become a tyrant, unless his powers are carefully limited. The Founders also knew that, although local governments are capable of tyranny, the risk is less severe than it is at the national level. That's because local governments operate closer to the people, making them more responsive to the people's needs and desires.

The founding generation learned this lesson firsthand as subjects of British rule. When we broke free from Great Britain, we weren't merely rebelling against the British monarchy or its specific abuses such as taxation without representation. As evidenced by the Declaration of Independence and other founding documents, the American Revolution rejected the very concept of an oppressive national government that recognized neither limits to its own power nor its people's right to local self-rule.

As a check against tyranny, the Founders created an exceptionally weak national government after the Revolution. That government, brought forth by the ill-fated Articles of Confederation, proved so weak that it could not address national problems. For example, the Articles of Confederation gave Congress the power to provide for national defense, but withheld the power to raise the money needed to fund defense operations. Likewise, Congress had no power to regulate interstate and foreign trade, rendering it powerless to stop the states from skirmishing over tariffs.

Recognizing these grave problems but still wary of a large, powerful national government, the Founding Fathers gathered in Philadelphia in the summer of 1787, ostensibly to amend the Articles of Confederation and, at a minimum, to empower Congress to regulate interstate trade. But by the end of that fateful summer they had instead produced a completely new constitution that expanded the power of the federal government, but did so within carefully defined boundaries. Under the Constitution, the federal government would exercise sovereign, supreme authority in specified areas in which *only* a national government could operate effectively. In all other areas, the states would retain sovereignty.

Nearly every power granted to the federal government can be found in Article I, Section 8 of the Constitution. That article empowers Congress to tax and borrow money; regulate interstate and foreign trade; establish uniform laws for immigration and naturalization, bankruptcy, weights and measures, trademarks, copyrights, and patents; coin money and regulate its value; establish post offices and post roads; establish federal courts; provide for national defense; grant letters of marque and reprisal;[1] declare war; and serve as the sole, sovereign lawmaker over land purchased by the United States with the consent of the host state.

Significantly, the Constitution does *not* grant Congress the power to pass any and every piece of legislation it deems necessary to make life "better" or more "fair." Nor can it fairly be read to empower Congress to:

- nationalize our nation's healthcare, car manufacturing, or banking industries
- create a cradle-to-grave entitlement system
- tell American citizens where to go to the doctor and how to pay for it
- stamp out economic disparities among Americans by "spreading the wealth around" or by any other method

No matter how great the idea, and no matter how pressing the perceived need, Congress may not legislate in any area in which it is not explicitly authorized to act; power in all those areas is vested in the states. Although this point was implicit in the text of the original Constitution—and was clear to every delegate to the Constitutional Convention of 1787 and to the vast majority of participants in the ensuing state ratification debates—it was made explicit by the Tenth Amendment, which was ratified two years after the Constitution took effect.

Those charged with wielding federal power in all three branches of government generally respected these limitations for roughly 150 years after the Constitution was written, executed, and ratified. There were, of course, disagreements about the precise extent of the limited powers granted to Congress, and there was a major clash over federal power with respect to a single issue—slavery—that was ultimately resolved by constitutional amendments adopted after the Civil War. But few doubted the importance of maintaining a clear distinction between state power and federal power. Nor was it considered the least bit controversial to say that, while the powers of Congress are few and defined, the powers of the states are numerous and indefinite.

Indeed, for those 150 years, members of Congress frequently objected to proposed legislation on the grounds that the Constitution afforded Congress no authority to enact it. Such objections were raised, often successfully, regardless of how laudable the proposals might be, and regardless of whether or not the president and the Supreme Court seemed inclined to turn a blind eye to Congress's power-grab.

Again, that is not to say all members of Congress always agreed on the precise extent of their power as federal lawmakers, or that Congress always saw eye to eye with the president and the Supreme Court on that question. In many areas, the Constitution's wording is broad enough that reasonable minds can disagree on the limits of federal power.

My point is that until the New Deal, such questions *were addressed*, resulting in an invaluable process that I call "the constitutional debate." The fact that this discussion occurred not just within the judiciary, but within the executive and legislative branches as well, showed that limits on federal power were a vital part of our national political discourse. Federal officials in all three branches of government understood that, consistent with their oaths to uphold the Constitution, they had an obligation to protect the rights of their fellow citizens by, among other things, safeguarding limits on federal power—regardless of whether they thought their colleagues and counterparts in other branches would restrain themselves in like fashion.

As long as the constitutional debate continued, the government maintained the critical balance between state and federal power. This meant that the states spent most of the money and exercised most of the power associated with government, in line with constitutional norms. And although this system did not produce *perfect* government, it undoubtedly protected Americans from the form of tyranny most feared by the Founding Fathers: an all-powerful national sovereign.

Despite their various failings, America's federal government and its state governments maintained the constitutional debate up to the 1930s, thus protecting individual liberty and perpetuating constitutionally limited government. With the arrival of the New Deal, however, this delicate balance was permanently upended.

★ ★ ★

Our drift away from the constitutional debate—and with it, from constitutionally limited government—began during the Great Depression. By the early 1930s, we were desperately seeking a way out of the devastating malaise that was crippling our economy and threatening our way of life.

In short, Americans were looking for a hero to save us. And for a hero to emerge, he typically needs two things: a widely despised villain to defeat, and access to the resources and power needed to crush that villain and reverse the evil deeds he committed.

In time, Americans identified the villain of the Great Depression as Herbert Hoover, a Republican president whose progressive dalliances had utterly failed to steer the country clear of economic disaster. Far from a limited-government conservative, as he is often portrayed to this day, Hoover tried to end the Depression by expanding the role of the federal government via dramatic tax hikes, damaging trade restrictions, and new spending programs to subsidize infrastructure projects, banks, and other businesses.

When these efforts failed to turn the economy around, many influential Americans refused to concede that expanding the federal government might be the wrong approach. Instead, Hoover was widely condemned for not expanding the government *enough*. He became a veritable hate figure, condemned both for his actions and his alleged motives. He was blamed personally for causing the entire global Depression—quite an achievement for a president whose scant powers paled in comparison to those of his successors. And Hoover's villainy is still an article of faith today, as seen in everything from our continued description of homeless encampments as "Hoovervilles" to catchy songs condemning the ill-fated Republican in the Broadway musical *Annie*.

I am not seeking to resurrect Hoover's reputation, but simply noting that his vilification set the stage for the nation to heroize some other man who could defeat Hoover and undo the damage he had supposedly wrought. Americans soon identified their would-be hero as Franklin D. Roosevelt, who beat Hoover in the 1932 election and then set out to end the Depression through an unprecedented expansion in the size, scope, and reach of the federal government.

FDR sought to expand Congress's power by relying on a fantastically broad reading of the Constitution's Commerce Clause (Article I, Section 8, Clause 3), which empowers Congress to regulate trade between the states and with foreign nations. The Roosevelt administration insisted this clause empowered Congress to regulate many local, purely intrastate activities—in realms such as labor, manufacturing, and agriculture—if their aggregate effect impacted interstate commerce even *indirectly*. A transaction could thus be classified as interstate commerce even if it did not use channels and instrumentalities of interstate commerce such as interstate roadways, waterways, airways, and airwaves.

With an overwhelming Democratic majority in Congress— aided by a supportive chorus of journalists, academics, and big businesses—FDR encountered little resistance in Washington in implementing his New Deal agenda.

★ ★ ★

Initially, the Supreme Court acted as the one significant impediment to FDR and Congress as they asserted powers that had traditionally been reserved to the states and, more importantly, were not within the limited, enumerated powers granted Congress by the Constitution.

The Court outlined its reasoning in its ruling in *Schechter Poultry Corp. v. United States* (1935), which invalidated federal legislation regulating the wages and hours of poultry industry workers. While the Court recognized that it is not always easy to clearly define Congress's authority under the Commerce Clause, it held that "the authority of the federal government may not be pushed to such an extreme as to destroy the distinction, which the commerce clause itself establishes, between commerce 'among the several States' and the internal concerns of a State." The Court further recognized that, regardless of how broadly or narrowly Congress might view its Commerce Clause authority, it cannot exercise that authority so extensively that "the federal authority would embrace practically all the activities of the people, and the authority of the State over its domestic concerns would exist only by sufferance of the federal government."

Applying this constitutional reasoning without judging the merits of the legislation, the Court ruled in several key cases that New Deal programs needed to be pursued in the state legislatures rather than in Congress. For example, in *Carter v. Carter Coal Company* (1936), the Court struck down New Deal regulations of the mining industry, arguing that mining is a local, intrastate activity that cannot be regulated as interstate commerce.

Buoyed by his status as a national hero (especially among his backers in the media), FDR sought to eliminate the Supreme Court's crucial check on federal authority through his infamous court-packing scheme—a congressional proposal that would have authorized him to appoint a new justice to the Supreme Court for each justice over the age of seventy. The bill would have empowered FDR to appoint as many as six sympathetic justices during his second term in office, all but assuring that the Court would green-light his agenda.

Although the court-packing bill died in Congress, one could argue that it achieved its objective. In 1937, two Supreme Court justices—Associate Justice Owen Roberts and Chief Justice Charles Evans Hughes—abandoned their opposition to FDR's expansionist view of the Commerce Clause and joined three others—Associate Justices Louis Brandeis, Harlan Stone, and Benjamin Cardozo—who had already embraced it. This created a five-member majority that, in *National Labor Relations Board v. Jones & Laughlin Steel Corp* (1937), upheld the National Labor Relations Act of 1935 even though the bill, like so many other New Deal laws, regulated a purely local, intrastate activity (labor) that affected interstate commerce only indirectly. While it is hard to determine precisely what prompted Roberts and Hughes to change their positions, one could reasonably surmise they feared that, unless they relented, FDR would eventually curtail their power by pushing a new court-packing proposal, mandating their early retirement, or finding some other way to undermine their authority.

★ ★ ★

From that moment forward, the Supreme Court became a rubber stamp for FDR's agenda. The high-water mark, from which the Court has not retreated to this day, was *Wickard v. Filburn* (1942), a case involving a farmer named Roscoe Filburn who committed what the Roosevelt administration considered a grave offense against humanity. What, you might ask, did Mr. Filburn do? Did he commit murder? Bank robbery? Arson?

No, Mr. Filburn's crime was growing too much wheat. You see, New Deal legislation allowed the federal government to limit the amount of wheat a farmer could grow each year. Because Filburn grew more wheat than the government, in its infinite wisdom, thought he should, he was ordered to pay a substantial fine. Filburn then challenged the government in court, arguing that Congress lacked the constitutional authority to limit wheat production. In its defense, the government insisted that because there is an established interstate market for wheat, and because wheat production affects interstate commerce, the government has the authority to limit wheat production under the Commerce Clause.

Filburn responded that the "excess" wheat he grew was both produced and consumed entirely within one state, that is, on his farm in Montgomery County, Ohio—he apparently used it as food for his family and livestock, while reserving the remainder to use as seed for future crop plantings.

The Supreme Court sided with the government, finding that "[h]ome-grown wheat ... competes with wheat in commerce," and that Congress "may properly have considered that wheat consumed on the farm where grown, if wholly outside the scheme of regulation, would have a substantial effect in defeating and obstructing its purpose to stimulate trade therein at increased prices." In other words, by consuming his own wheat on his own farm, Roscoe Filburn engaged in conduct that, when replicated across the country, would substantially affect the price of wheat.

That, the Court decided, rendered Filburn's local, intrastate activity subject to Congress's power to regulate interstate commerce. As long as the regulated activity "exerts a substantial economic effect on interstate commerce," the Court ruled, it is subject to federal control—"irrespective of whether such effect is what might at some earlier time have been defined as 'direct' or 'indirect.'"

Wickard v. Filburn had sweeping implications. In light of that decision—which has never been reversed—Congress may, without interference from the courts, use the Commerce Clause to regulate any activity that, when measured in the aggregate, substantially affects interstate commerce. Under that standard, almost every human endeavor, even non-economic activity, is potentially subject to federal regulation under the Commerce Clause.

With this ruling, the Supreme Court sent Congress an unmistakable message: "Feel free to do whatever you want under the Commerce Clause; we won't second-guess your judgment." In the wake of *Wickard*, members of Congress stopped asking the question of whether they *could* regulate anything because the default answer was a resounding "yes." They stopped asking whether they *could*, and then eventually stopped asking whether they *should*. And thus the constitutional debate in Congress— and along with it, the time-honored, constitutional concept of limited federal power—steadily faded into obscurity.

★ ★ ★

Only twice since the 1942 *Wickard* ruling has the Supreme Court concluded that an act of Congress failed this loose standard of review: in *United States v. Lopez* (1995), the Court invalidated a portion of the Gun-Free School Zones Act of 1990 that criminalized the bare, non-commercial possession of a gun within the vicinity of a school; and in *United States v. Morrison* (2000), the Court invalidated a section of the Violence Against Women Act of 1994 that gave victims of gender-motivated violent crimes the right to sue their attackers in federal court. One could cynically but credibly argue that in both cases, the Court did little more than reprimand Congress for sloppy draftsmanship, while offering instructions on how it could re-enact similar legislation without running afoul of the (largely theoretical) limits on federal power under the Commerce Clause.

Thanks to the Court's Commerce Clause jurisprudence, the constitutional debate in Congress today is anemic at best. Members of Congress decide each statute's constitutionality simply by asking whether it will likely withstand review in court. Instead of consulting the Constitution—the fundamental document they have sworn to uphold—members of Congress tend to rely on the judgment of nine lifetime-appointed, robe-wearing legal experts who work in the white marble palace across the street from the Capitol. Due in part to this line of cases, most members of Congress ask not what the Constitution actually says or how it was understood by those who drafted and ratified it, but rather what they can get away with in court.

As long as that remains true, and until the Court begins strictly interpreting the Commerce Clause and enforcing its limits, constitutionally limited government will exist only in theory. But restoring the constitutional debate could take decades, and we can't wait that long. The unfettered expansion of the federal government is worsening our debt problem by increasing the cost of the federal government and by impeding free-market forces, making it harder for the economy to generate enough tax revenue to fund federal operations. At a time when we have accumulated more than $14 trillion in debt and are adding $1.65 trillion to that debt every year, we must act now to restrain federal power. And if the Supreme Court won't do it, then the American people should, by demanding a balanced budget amendment.

CHAPTER THREE

★ ★ ★

Restoring the Constitutional Debate

If we want to cut our federal government down to its proper size, we have to vote differently. We simply can't afford to continue re-electing members of Congress who interpret the Commerce Clause in a way that obliterates the crucial distinction between federal power (which is limited) and state power (which is relatively open-ended). We have to repopulate Congress with men and women who understand the state-federal distinction and will fight to defend it.

Specifically, we as citizens need to do three things:

- Learn the language of limited government found in the Constitution.

- Share that knowledge with our freedom-loving friends and family members.
- Hold our elected representatives accountable when they fail to respect that language.

In other words, we need to restore the constitutional debate to Congress, one senator and one representative at a time.

Although this task may sound daunting, in fact it is remarkably simple. We must demand that members of Congress tell us where they get their authority to enact each and every piece of legislation they support. Whenever a congressman or senator can't answer that simple question with an equally simple, plain-spoken explanation consistent with the text and original understanding of the Constitution, then regardless of what Supreme Court precedent might tell Congress it can get away with, we should make clear that we expect him to vote against the bill. And whenever a member of Congress refuses to comply with that expectation, we should strive to replace that member with someone who will serve as a consistent advocate for constitutionally limited government.

We should also seek to replace any member of Congress who refuses to keep the federal government focused on the national issues that only it can address. We must, of course, remember that these limited responsibilities are explicitly defined by the Constitution.

The problem we face is neither esoteric nor contrived; the more time Congress spends trying to do things it is *not* authorized to do, the less time it spends solving the important problems that fall within its rightful jurisdiction. For example, when Congress becomes consumed with trying to tell Americans where to go to the doctor and how to pay for medical services, it can't focus as effectively on issues like border security and national defense.

You don't need to have a law degree or a Ph.D. to pursue this strategy aggressively and effectively. Nor do you have to devote your entire life to politics. All you have to do is read about the issues and then vote for public officials who convince you, through both word and deed, of their fealty to limited government. While your own vote is vital, it is also imperative to draw more people to the cause by speaking to others about the importance of limited government and how its restoration will help solve our national debt crisis.

★ ★ ★

The effort to restore constitutionally limited government will draw its share of opponents, since we are calling for a dramatic shift in the way our federal government functions. This kind of fundamental reform often fosters uncertainty, fear, and even hostility. But that doesn't mean we shouldn't try; it just means we must prepare ourselves to respond effectively to those who will fight us every step of the way.

Opponents of constitutionally limited government typically resort to three main arguments. The first is that restoring constitutional boundaries between federal and state governments requires changes that would offset or reverse civil rights liberties gained since the 1960s. Proponents of this argument usually contend that Congress could not have enacted the Civil Rights Act of 1964 had it not relied on the Supreme Court's expansionist reading of the Commerce Clause.

That is incorrect. In enacting the Civil Rights Act, Congress could have (and I believe should have) relied on Section 5 of the Fourteenth Amendment, which expressly authorizes Congress to "enforce this article [including the Fourteenth Amendment's Equal Protection Clause, Due Process Clause, and Privileges and Immunities Clause] by appropriate legislation." This grant of authority is clearly broad enough to sustain legislation prohibiting, among other things, racial and gender discrimination in employment, housing, and education. But Congress instead relied on the Commerce Clause, demonstrating that the Supreme Court has made that clause such an easy-to-use, one-size-fits-all tool that Congress prefers to invoke it even when another approach is more appropriate.

Second, many argue that states, local governments, and individuals have become so dependent on federal subsidies and services that our economy could not survive without those programs. Since many of those programs would be eliminated if we returned to constitutionally limited government, they claim, we have no choice but to retain our current big-government structure.

While this argument dramatically overstates the case, it does have an element of truth—the elimination of a large number of federal spending programs would cause considerable challenges to individuals and states alike. But the fact that we, as a nation, have become dependent on those programs is hardly a reason to keep them forever. To the contrary, considering that dependence on government is a common tool used for perpetuating tyranny, our dangerous level of government dependence today ought to strengthen our resolve to reassert our personal sovereignty and end these federal programs once and for all.

To minimize the disruption of our transition to limited government, we can take a phased approached. Many federal programs and services are wasteful, duplicative, ineffective, or totally unnecessary, having arisen to satisfy some politician's political demands rather than to meet any widespread, pressing need on the part of the American people. Those programs can be eliminated quickly. Other federal programs that actually meet legitimate needs can be scaled down gradually, with responsibility turned over to state and local governments. These governments can administer these programs more effectively anyway, because they can tailor them to meet their residents' unique demands.

The third common argument against restoring limited government is that, if the federal government transfers responsibility over various programs to the states, then some states will end up offering more robust entitlement benefits than others. This is undoubtedly true, but it's actually a *positive* result of this transformation—in fact, it's one of the core arguments for the system of federalism our Founders designed. Residents of one state might want a more robust entitlement system, while those of another state might choose lower taxes over more benefits. People who prefer one of those systems over the other could then choose to live in the state that best meets their needs.

What that really means is that Americans would have more options. States would compete with each other to develop the best system that would attract the most residents and businesses. For the same reason that competition in any industry results in better products and improved service, competition among governments leads to innovation, improved efficiency, and greater responsiveness to the voters.

That's why the Founding Fathers thought of the states as "laboratories of republican democracy." They understood that by vesting most power in the states, they would leave each state free to design its own policies according to local needs. Healthy competition would improve all the states' systems, while states could borrow successful reforms from other states and refrain from experiments that didn't work elsewhere. This system of experimentation and choice, however, is severely impeded today, as the federal government—which doesn't face any competition at all—usurps more and more authority from the states.

Notwithstanding the criticisms of our opponents, our movement enjoys a great advantage: the Constitution already provides us with a framework for accomplishing what we need to do. And it's clear the push for restoring limited government will have to be a bottom-up, grassroots effort. Having facilitated our drift away from the Constitution, the courts can't be relied upon to bring us back—only through the electoral process can we restore what has been lost. Most important, as we return power to the states, we will return power to the American people.

Now we will turn our attention to the linchpin of the limited government movement. While electing officials who respect the language of the Constitution is a critical first step, history shows that even the most sincere defenders of the Constitution can, over time, give in to the constant demands for bigger, more powerful, more intrusive government. The Founders understood it is simply human nature for government officials—elected and unelected alike—to seek to expand their own power, and the Founders wrote an intricate system of checks and balances into the Constitution to restrain precisely this impulse. Unfortunately, as evidenced by our ever-growing, increasingly powerful federal government and the catastrophic debt it has compiled, that system has proven inadequate. It is now time to correct that system through a balanced budget amendment.

PART II

★ ★ ★

How Efforts to Balance the Budget Will Help Restore Constitutionally Limited Government

★ ★ ★

CHAPTER FOUR

A Time to Amend

As a staunch advocate of a balanced budget amendment, I am sometimes asked, "How can you profess to be a champion of the Constitution when you want to amend it?" Although the question almost answers itself, it reflects a fairly widespread uncertainty about constitutional norms.

Amending the Constitution, of course, is a serious matter that cannot be approached cavalierly. That said, we must remember that the Founding Fathers foresaw the need to amend the Constitution from time to time and supplied future generations with procedures for doing so. Using those methods, Americans have adopted a total of twenty-seven constitutional amendments, many of which have proven not only beneficial, but essential to the survival of our republic and to the values upon which it was established.

For example, about two years after the Constitution was ratified, we adopted the first ten amendments which, among other things, prohibit Congress from enacting laws restricting free speech, interfering with the free exercise of religion, subjecting citizens to unreasonable searches and seizures, subjecting citizens to a trial without a jury and competent legal counsel, taking private property without due process and just compensation, and subjecting a convicted criminal to cruel and unusual punishment. Few Americans, if any, would dispute that these amendments have safeguarded individual liberty and have served as effective bulwarks against tyranny.

Likewise, at the conclusion of the Civil War, we adopted the Thirteenth, Fourteenth, and Fifteenth Amendments which, among other things, outlaw slavery and prohibit the states from denying anyone the right to vote or otherwise discriminating on the basis of race or color.

These and other amendments have made our country more free, more prosperous, more just, and more true to our common understanding, expressed in the Declaration of Independence, that "all men are created equal, that they are endowed by their Creator with certain unalienable Rights, [and] that among these are Life, Liberty and the pursuit of Happiness." Indeed, America would be a much different country without our constitutional amendments—and now it is time to amend once again.

This book will soon discuss how a balanced budget amendment should be drafted and what specific restrictions it should impose on congressional spending. But first, in this chapter, let's look at the reasons why Congress has become fundamentally *incapable* of fiscal responsibility, and why attempts to enforce spending discipline on it and to restore constitutionally limited government will ultimately fall short absent a balanced budget amendment.

★ ★ ★

Article I, Section 8, Clause 2 of the Constitution gives Congress the power "[t]o borrow money on the credit of the United States." Intended to give Congress flexibility for spending during wars and other national emergencies, this power has been abused so severely for so long that we have no choice but to strictly limit its application. Having accumulated a staggering debt exceeding $14 trillion, Congress is clearly unable to wield the debt-accrual power responsibly.

Lest we overlook how much money is at stake (which many members of Congress desperately want us to do), we must recall that each American's per capita share of our national debt amounts to about $50,000, such that a family of five can be said to own a portion of the national debt valued at roughly *a quarter million dollars*. And given that only about half of all wage earners are required to pay federal income tax, those who do pay such taxes may well own a share of the national debt that is *several times larger* than that.

Even worse, many of those who will have to repay this debt are not old enough to vote, while others have yet to be born. We may be paying the bill for Congress's spending spree for generations to come, meaning many of those responsible for accumulating this massive debt will no longer be in office to face the full consequences of their foolish actions. I don't know any other circumstance in which an American citizen can inherit a debt, small or large, that was incurred not only without his consent, but prior to his birth.

Most people would agree that all citizens who have to repay a massive government debt should, at a minimum, have an opportunity to voice their concerns about it to their elected representatives before the debt is incurred. But that is impossible when we're dealing with this kind of inter-generational debt. Thus, the more debt today's officials accumulate, and the longer they wait before repaying it, the less accountable they will be to those most adversely affected by it.

In this respect, perpetual deficit spending results in a form of taxation without representation. A major cause of the American Revolution, unjust taxation is incompatible with the very concept of a free nation—and it is no more acceptable when imposed by the American Congress than when it was practiced by the British Empire.

Thankfully, unlike the problem our Founders faced, our current debt crisis can be resolved peacefully. But in order to achieve a peaceful resolution, we must first understand *why* Congress is irresistibly attracted to perpetual deficit spending.

Members of Congress face an overwhelming, five-fold set of circumstances tempting them to engage in reckless spending. As they spend *trillions* of dollars each year, members of Congress are:

- prompted by a genuine desire to leave a tangible mark on society and otherwise make the world a better place

- motivated by a desire for praise and adoration, informed by the understanding that spending *more* generally leads to public praise while spending *less* leads to public criticism
- spending on a massive scale that tends to distort their sense of perspective
- operating without any clear parameters delineating the boundaries of their substantive authority
- spending without any real limit on the amount of money they have at their disposal

The first four conditions can be mitigated, but they can't be eliminated completely—and as explained below, in some cases we would not want to eliminate them. Thus, even as we take what steps we can to impose restraint on Congress, we have to acknowledge that these will only be short-term fixes until we ratify a balanced budget amendment. As for the fifth condition, that can be resolved *only* by a balanced budget amendment. In the following pages, I will address each condition in turn.

The Laudable Desire to Do Good Things

The first factor, the desire to improve the human condition, is as laudable as it is fundamental to human nature. We can't neutralize the desire to make the world a better place; nor would we want to elect members of Congress who lack that inclination. But we can and should help our representatives understand that increased federal spending is not always the best means of improving the world, and that comparable or even greater benefits can often be achieved through spending *cuts* that leave more money in the taxpayers' pockets.

Members of Congress tend to address every problem by throwing money at it, since that's an easy "achievement" they can tout as evidence that they care about the issue. Even if the problem never gets solved or even grows worse, congressmen will boast about how they voted to spend millions of dollars on a "solution."

What I'm really criticizing is not the desire to make the world a better place, but rather the assumption among members of Congress that spending more money is always the best way to do it. They may have worthy motives, but this assumption gives rise to a dangerous impulse, especially because the spending "solution" is typically the easiest one to explain and implement, even if it threatens to cause more problems than it resolves.

Aside from prompting the initial impulse to spend, the desire to make the world a better place also tends to ease the consciences of elected officials who—if not convinced they were improving the lives of deserving people—might otherwise hesitate to mortgage the futures of our next generations. To be sure, their belief that their profligate spending is helping good, deserving people is not entirely delusional; in some way, every government program benefits someone, and some of them support millions of people. That makes politicians happy—not just because it makes them popular and more electable, but because nearly all politicians genuinely want to help people.

But one crucial question is rarely asked: does the benefit provided by each program justify that program's cost to future taxpayers? We will never know what great inventions, discoveries, or other accomplishments our descendants might otherwise have achieved if not for the crushing debt we are passing along to them.

Future generations should be free to decide how much faith to put in government programs, just as our generation made that decision for ourselves. To preserve that choice for our children and grandchildren, we have to remind members of Congress that, in contemplating how to improve society, they have to consider the potential negative effects—even catastrophic effects—their spending decisions will have on America's future.

These entreaties can have an effect—especially if they're backed up by votes—but it will be limited. The desire to do good will always tempt politicians to spend more money, and we cannot expect to eliminate that desire—we can control it only by imposing strict constitutional restraints.

The Quest to Bask in Praise and Avoid Criticism

Elected officials inevitably seek to earn praise and avoid criticism. We should attempt to temper and offset this instinct, recognizing that the public (spurred by the news media) tends to heap praise on big-spending politicians while criticizing the Grinches who advocate spending restraint. However, similar to politicians' desire to do good things, we have to acknowledge that we will never eliminate this desire entirely.

Let's face it—it's fun to give people what they want. And giving makes the giver popular and more inclined to give even more, especially when (a) the act of giving requires little or no sacrifice by the giver, because he is giving something that doesn't belong to him, and (b) the gift's recipients ask for the gift with far more urgency and unity than those who oppose it.

"Giving" in those circumstances tends to produce a cycle in which the politician receives praise and acquires popularity, enjoys it, and seeks out more opportunities for further giving, knowing it will result in more praise and popularity. Meanwhile, the politician knows that if he reduces his giving, his former beneficiaries will denounce him as strongly as they had previously praised him.

To counter this tendency, Americans need to remind politicians that spending public money is a double-edged sword; while many people benefit from federal programs enabled by huge deficit spending, many others—including some who are not yet born—will be required to sacrifice much to pay for those programs. Elected officials must also be reminded that, although money expended through a government program will inevitably produce demonstrable benefits, it is often true that the same money might well produce *greater* benefits if left in the hands of the people who earned it.

For example, many pundits argue that in a recession Congress should appropriate hundreds of billions of dollars to fund large-scale public-works projects that will "stimulate" the economy. What goes unmentioned is that the same money, had it not been confiscated by the government, would have at some point been spent elsewhere, stimulating the private-sector economy as much as—and likely more than—any government program ever could. That doesn't mean public-works programs are never a good idea; it just means we should not fund these programs simply as a means of improving a sluggish economy.

Some observers counter that in a recession money simply isn't moving, meaning the money allocated to a proposed public-works program simply would not be spent unless the government borrowed and spent it. However, money doesn't stop moving through the economy without a reason—and the government often is the reason. The American people themselves will invest, start and grow businesses, create jobs, expand wealth, and otherwise contribute to economic growth if they can reasonably expect to enjoy the fruits of their labors. Severe recessions occur whenever that expectation is diminished, as is typically the case when the government expands its financial footprint.

Therefore, combating a recession by expanding government intrusion in the economy, either through deficit spending or otherwise, is a fool's errand. By this logic, an alcoholic suffering from cirrhosis of the liver should go on a therapeutic drinking binge whenever his symptoms flare up.

While intuitive and relatively easy to explain, voters rarely communicate the economic benefits of spending restraint to their elected officials. That needs to change, and the movement for constitutionally limited government is the perfect vehicle for ushering in that change. Once we incorporate these free-market principles into our national political discourse, politicians will begin seeking praise via fiscal responsibility instead of through reckless spending.

Congress Spends on a Massive Scale

One of the little-noted reasons for Congress's profligacy is that, to use the language of the retail consumer, Congress "buys" everything in bulk. You're probably thinking, "But buying in bulk saves money." That's generally true, but bulk buying can easily lead to excessive spending if it's not managed carefully— and in Congress, it is *not* managed carefully.

Let's consider this on a personal level. I love shopping at huge, no-frills warehouses like Costco, where you can buy almost anything—from cotton swabs to televisions, from candy to toothbrushes, from caskets to tablecloths—in bulk, with bulk-rate pricing. But when I shop there I end up buying things I never thought I needed, often in huge quantities. I suspect I'm not alone in that habit, and I also suspect Costco executives know I'm not alone. They have mastered bulk-buying psychology in order to persuade their customers to spend lots of money.

Costco managers seem to understand that a customer typi-cally spends *more* money when he's bulk buying than when he's shopping at a traditional retail store. That's because it's easier for the Costco customer to lose his sense of scale—in other words, his perspective on how much he's spending—and to overlook the fact that he might be buying far more than he really needs.

Suppose, for example, that I needed to buy paper towels. If I bought them at a grocery store, I would probably spend two or three dollars buying one or two rolls. But if I bought them at Costco, I would buy at least twelve rolls, spending almost twenty dollars. Even though the price per roll is lower at Costco, I would still be spending more money there on a single purchase than I would at the grocery store. Perhaps buying paper towels in bulk is worth it because I would eventually use all twelve rolls, but spending that much money on paper towels could affect my general spending psychology, distorting my sense of scale and leading to excessive spending on other items.

Committing to spend twenty dollars on paper towels would make me more prone to spend fifteen dollars on a big bottle of olive oil or pure maple syrup or a bag of frozen ravioli—even though I would never buy those products (at least not at those prices) at the grocery store. When I find myself mentally "in the Costco zone," it's easy for me to forget that I rarely pay more than ten dollars for any household product at the grocery store.

This example helps to explain why Congress has spent so much money for so long. Especially at the national level, elected politicians quickly become accustomed to spending on such a large scale that they tend to lose perspective. For most members of Congress, after just a few weeks in office a billion dollars begins to seem like a relatively modest sum. Consequently, many of them won't even flinch when asked to support an appropriation of "only" $500,000, $5 million, or even $50 million. Such amounts actually seem quite small compared to the giant spending bills they've already approved—and besides, it isn't their money they're spending.

Worse still, members of Congress are faced with a strange "bulk purchasing" requirement that would never work at Costco or anywhere else in the private sector. In some instances, members of Congress cannot vote to fund a government program they support (let's say, medical benefits for veterans) without voting to fund a whole host of other programs, some of which they may oppose (for example, funding for Planned Parenthood). This dilemma results from the use of omnibus spending bills—long pieces of legislation that simultaneously fund hundreds or even thousands of distinct spending programs.

There are, of course, legitimate reasons for Congress to use omnibus bills. Adopting any piece of legislation, especially funding legislation, requires painstaking compromise and negotiation. And to gain support to fund one critical program, leaders in Congress often have to agree to support funding for other, less critical programs. Additionally, the federal government is so large and its annual budget so complex that simple time constraints make omnibus spending packages an attractive option.

Nevertheless, when you consider how this practice would play out on a personal level, the problem with omnibus bills becomes painfully evident. Imagine that you go to the grocery store to buy bread, milk, and eggs, and that you live in a remote location without access to any other store. Now, imagine further that as you approach the cash register you are bluntly informed that you may not make your purchase unless—in addition to bread, milk, and eggs—you also buy a hammer, a copy of Barry Manilow's hit 1975 album *Tryin' to Get the Feeling*, a half-ton of iron ore, and a book of cowboy poetry.

After adjusting to the initial shock of this bizarre arrangement, you would at some point realize you had no choice but to accept it. Because of your non-negotiable need for food staples and your lack of access to other options, you'd be forced to buy things you didn't want or need. Over time, this arrangement would increase the cost of everything you bought, potentially causing you to go deeply into debt.

As strange as this scenario may sound, it isn't all that different from the gut-wrenching choices members of Congress sometimes face when confronted with omnibus spending bills. House and Senate leaders often claim those bills are necessary to "get things done" or to "make Congress more efficient." Few people object to anything promoting such lofty-sounding objectives, even though this approach often coerces otherwise-reluctant members into voting to fund one thing simply because they want to fund another. This practice has significantly increased federal spending as well as our national debt.

There is no easy solution to this problem. The compromises and negotiations needed to keep the legislative process moving will always result in spending packages that fund numerous programs. But some of the damage could be mitigated if members of Congress, at the urging of their constituents, would make "no" their default vote on all spending measures. In other words, constituents should demand that their senators and representatives stop approving spending bills simply because they contain certain items they support; if the bill contains other things they *don't* support, they should vote against it.

Of course, in light of today's historic level of government spending, employing this strategy could erode a politician's popularity as he votes against funding deemed essential to his state or district. Nevertheless, many members of Congress would adhere to this strategy if a large, vocal segment of their constituency demanded it and voted on the issue.

Just as no one would tolerate a grocery store requiring us to buy certain products as a condition for buying others, we should not tolerate a system that forces members of Congress to spend this way. Although it may be impossible to dismantle that system entirely, voters can chip away at it by demanding that their senators and representatives make their default vote on spending measures a resounding "no."

Congress's Limitless Authority

As explained in previous chapters, in recent decades members of Congress have largely abandoned the constitutional debate and have ceased to enforce limits on their own authority, instead assuming they may enact any piece of legislation capable of surviving the Supreme Court's permissive, deferential standards of review. For now, our best hope for reversing this trend, and for making government more responsive and less cumbersome, is to restore the constitutional debate and remind members of Congress that their legislative power is limited

If, for example, members of Congress recognized that they have no authority to micromanage the healthcare decisions of over 300 million U.S. citizens, then the Patient Protection and Affordable Care Act of 2010, a.k.a. "ObamaCare," would never have become law. And had Congress refused to pass ObamaCare, we could have avoided a new debt burden that will soon amount to *trillions of dollars.* This is just one of many examples demonstrating a simple principle: Congress spends more money when its members believe, however mistakenly, that they have authority to enact any piece of legislation that embodies what they see as a good idea.

As part of a growing backlash against out-of-control federal spending, dozens of limited-government adherents have been elected to Congress in recent years. I am pleased to count myself as one of them. Our numbers and seniority don't yet permit us to make constitutionally limited government the standard in every instance, but our mere presence has already begun to change the political discourse.

We need reinforcements. Grassroots activists need to recruit supporters of limited government and help get them elected. The more widespread the constitutional debate becomes in Congress, the more effective we will be in restoring our nation's fiscal health.

Congress Draws from a Limitless Well of Money

Focusing on the four factors listed above will help reorient the federal government toward fiscal restraint. But these habits are so deeply entrenched in Congress that changing them will not definitively solve our economic crisis. Congress may take some meaningful steps toward reducing the deficit and perhaps even produce a balanced budget, but in the long run the old spendthrift habits will re-emerge—they always do. So after we change the culture of over-spending in Congress, we have to ensure that it *stays* changed. We do that by addressing the fifth factor in congressional over-spending—the fact that deficit spending gives Congress access to an unlimited amount of money. A single step will permanently solve this problem: enacting a balanced budget amendment to the Constitution.

This is a vital reform that cannot be delayed any longer. Congress's spending binge is increasing the power and intrusiveness of the federal government at the expense of the American people. Each dollar borrowed by Congress makes every American incrementally less prosperous and less free. With this soft, gradual slide into tyranny, future Americans will be born less free than their parents and grandparents were, based on decisions made by leaders who were elected, served, and died before they were born.

Fortunately, the scope of Congress's authority to borrow is something we can change, and a properly drafted balanced budget amendment would do precisely that. The next chapter will outline the key elements of a balanced budget amendment that would end Congress's perpetual deficit spending once and for all.

CHAPTER FIVE

★ ★ ★

Critical Elements of a Balanced Budget Amendment

W e can begin to restore constitutionally limited government by insisting that Congress balance its budget each year.

For Congress, money and power are inextricably linked: the more money the government has, the more power it gets—and as it acquires more power, it demands more money. This dynamic cycle is likely to end in a soft form of tyranny, especially when it's perpetuated by a government, like our current federal government, that recognizes no real limit on its power, and that engages in perpetual deficit spending in a way that effectively removes any real limit on the amount of money it can spend.

The most practical and effective way to end this cycle is to impose permanent structural limits on the government's power to borrow and spend. Specifically, the best solution is a constitutional amendment that requires Congress to balance its budget each year, subject only to limited, narrow, and difficult-to-invoke exceptions. That amendment will put the federal government on a restricted fiscal diet, thereby restoring constitutionally limited government—and along with it, freedom and prosperity.

★ ★ ★

If we take the difficult, time-consuming step of adopting a balanced budget amendment, we need to ensure that it will actually fix the underlying problem and permanently end Congress's practice of perpetual deficit spending. Crucially, because Congress is likely to resist efforts to restrain its spending authority, an effective balanced budget amendment needs to impose myriad spending restraints that minimize the chance that any restrictions could be circumvented.

An ideal balanced budget amendment would contain at least five elements. While an amendment containing any of these elements would go a long way toward restoring the federal government's fiscal responsibility, one containing all five of them would almost certainly resolve our fiscal crisis permanently.

Element One: Equalize Revenues and Outlays

The first element would prohibit Congress from spending more during any fiscal year than the federal government "earns" during that year by collecting tax and other revenue. Stated differently, Congress would be required to adhere to a budget each year in which federal outlays do not exceed federal revenue. This is what most people think of when they hear the term "balanced budget amendment," and it closely resembles how most families, businesses, and state and local governments try to manage their finances. It is time that we demand nothing less from the federal government.

Unfortunately, such a requirement is far from foolproof. Under almost any practical scenario, this mandate would require Congress to rely on estimates in calculating the federal government's likely annual revenue (and to a lesser extent, likely outlays) for each fiscal year. Despite the efforts of our country's best accountants and economists, estimates are likely to be wrong from time to time, and they could also be deliberately manipulated in order to enhance Congress's spending power. Either way, we'll need a backup plan. That's where the other elements come into play.

Element Two: Spending May Not Exceed a Fixed Percentage of GDP

The second element would prohibit Congress from spending during any fiscal year more than a fixed percentage of the GDP of the previous calendar year. Although people may disagree on the proper percentage, I would put the figure at 18 percent. Over the last forty years, federal revenue has averaged roughly 18.5 percent of annual GDP, so a constitutional amendment imposing an "18 percent of GDP" limitation would require Congress to live within its long-term means, thereby preventing the inexorable expansion of federal spending relative to the size of the economy. (As of 2011, federal spending amounts to a staggering 25 percent of GDP; to put that in perspective, a century ago, both federal spending and federal revenue stood at just 2 percent.)

This limitation would stop Congress from manipulating revenue estimates. In fact, such estimates wouldn't be used at all, since the previous calendar year's GDP would be calculated before Congress adopted each year's budget—and that's a fixed number that could not be gamed after the fact.

That number could, however, be manipulated beforehand, by changing the data points that have historically been used to calculate GDP. But it would be relatively easy to detect that kind of machination and to identify those responsible for it. Once the data points have been ascertained for a particular year, GDP can accurately and reliably be determined. And given that the GDP figure in question relates to matters of historical fact, it would be difficult to manipulate.

Element Three: Supermajority Vote to Circumvent

The third element would provide that Congress could circumvent either of the two limitations discussed above only by a supermajority vote. We must recognize, as the Founding Fathers did, that extraordinary circumstances might arise from time to time that could require Congress to engage in short-term deficit spending. But such circumstances should be rare, and any exceptions to these restrictions need to be difficult to invoke.

This begs the question: what kind of supermajority vote—three-fifths, two-thirds, or three-fourths—should be required? I favor a two-thirds supermajority requirement, since that is the margin by which Congress must approve constitutional amendments and by which the Senate must ratify treaties. In my view, it should not be any easier for Congress to approve deficit spending than it is to approve a constitutional amendment or ratify a treaty. That said, I care less about the precise margin than I do about stopping Congress from approving deficit spending through a simple-majority vote.

Some believe we should make an exception to the supermajority-vote requirement for funding a declared war against a nation-state—that is, as opposed to a war against an abstract concept (like LBJ's "War on Poverty") or a non-state actor (such as al-Qaeda). According to this argument, once we declare war, we should respond in an overwhelming and unapologetic way, fighting relentlessly until victory without being hindered by short-term budgetary concerns. The Founding Fathers indeed had precisely this circumstance in mind when they gave Congress the right to incur debt in the first place.

The main point is this: if Congress understood at the outset of a war that it would be subject to the supermajority requirement for the war's duration, it would ensure that we would only engage in wars when there is a national consensus to do so, and that non-war spending would be minimized so that funds remained available for the fight.

However, I don't believe a balanced budget amendment must contain this kind of exception. It would be both highly unusual and politically foolish for Congress to declare war against a nation-state (which has not happened since 1941) without first securing overwhelming support, both in Congress and in the nation at large, to adequately fund the effort. And historically, even when we have gone to battle without a formal declaration of war, Congress has voted overwhelmingly to fund and otherwise support our troops.

Element Four: Supermajority Vote to Raise the Debt Ceiling

The fourth element would require Congress to approve any debt-ceiling increase by a supermajority vote. This requirement would serve as an additional protection against Congress resorting to statistical trickery to satisfy its budget-balancing requirements.

Even if Congress found a way to manipulate estimates of revenue, outlays, and GDP in order to feign compliance with the amendment, the scheme would inevitably result in additional debt. If Congress continued to acquire new debt in this manner, it would eventually hit a previously established debt ceiling. Raising the vote threshold for lifting the debt ceiling would complicate that endeavor and give Congress yet another reason to proceed with great caution.

Under the current requirement of a simple-majority vote, Congress has been far too willing to increase the debt ceiling, a maneuver that presidents and legislative leaders regularly secure through their jeremiads that failing to do so will lead to catastrophe. These claims, in fact, have an element of truth, in that uncertainty and disorder would likely ensue if Congress refused to raise the debt ceiling *without first changing the way it spends money*.[1] But these arguments overlook the myriad ways we can minimize that insecurity without reflexively raising the debt ceiling as a means of continually postponing necessary budget cuts.

The most risky aspect of not raising the debt ceiling is this: at a time when 43 percent of our annual budget relies on borrowed money, no one knows exactly what would happen if the government suddenly had to stop borrowing. Conventional wisdom holds that absent additional statutory direction from Congress, the president would—upon losing his authority to incur new debt—be left to decide how to fund a $3.85 trillion government with only $2.2 trillion (as is the case in 2011).

This worries many members of Congress, who might not see eye-to-eye with the president as to which programs and departments should be fully funded, which should be subject to reduced funding, and which should receive no funding until Congress either raises the debt ceiling or adopts a new budget. Would active-duty military personnel continue to receive paychecks? Would retirees continue to receive their Social Security checks? Would interest on existing debt continue to be paid? Those questions and countless others, it seems, would be left to the president's discretion.

Thus, it would be risky and even irresponsible for Congress to refuse to raise the debt ceiling as a means of "forcing" a balanced budget overnight. In addition to causing countless practical problems affecting hundreds of millions of Americans—and potentially every American—this course of action would vest in the president vast, imperial-like spending authority he could wield to serve his own political and policy interests.[2]

This helps to explain why Congress routinely votes to raise the debt ceiling: though irresponsible, the decision is perceived as less irresponsible than refusing to raise the debt ceiling and potentially plunging the entire federal government into chaos.

However, as bad as this outcome may be, the consequences of constantly raising the debt ceiling may now be even worse. The perception is spreading that America is a financially irresponsible country that will have to deliberately inflate its currency to pay off its ballooning national debt. As more people anticipate that outcome, potential investors will become more reluctant to loan us money. That means we will have to pay higher interest rates in order to continue borrowing. These elevated rates will then ripple through the economy, affecting everything from home mortgages to defense spending to Social Security and every other federal priority.

In sum, while Congress may need to raise the debt ceiling occasionally, it should be more difficult to do that. Requiring a supermajority vote would provide a corrective counterbalance that would account for the risks of perpetual deficit spending.

Element Five: Supermajority Vote to Increase Taxes

Finally, a balanced budget amendment should require a supermajority vote in Congress to approve any tax increases. Raising taxes, particularly in a struggling economy, would impair economic growth and thwart our efforts to balance the budget. That's because we can create a balanced budget only through both fiscal restraint and sustained economic growth—neither factor will suffice on its own.

The economy grows as people invest their money—that is, as they risk their money in an endeavor with the expectation of securing a favorable return. Wise investments boost salaries, create new jobs, and lead to even more investment. As long as the proper incentives are in place and government minimizes its role to tasks that only government can perform, the economy grows. And as our economy grows, the government collects more tax revenue even as tax rates remain constant.

Thus, investment leads to economic growth, and economic growth leads to additional tax revenue. No tax hike is required.

Many observers, particularly on the left, believe we can increase government tax revenue by raising tax rates. That strategy, they claim, would allow us to balance the budget faster while reducing the need for drastic spending cuts. They further argue that the tax increase could be targeted only against the wealthy who can best afford it.

However, the "soak the rich" approach has proven to be economically disastrous. Whenever a tax structure provides enough revenue to fund law enforcement, defense, and other essential government operations, raising taxes will, to one degree or another, impede economic growth. That's because higher taxes undermine private investors' expectation that they can earn a good return on their investment. As they invest less, economic growth diminishes. Unlike other variables (such as fluctuations in the price of a particular commodity) that might threaten to lower an investor's anticipated return, tax hikes do more than threaten that return; they predictably erode it with stunning consistency and mathematical precision.

This is no less true of tax increases that purport to target only the wealthy. By definition, the wealthy have more money than the non-wealthy. For exactly that reason, they are more likely than others to invest, create jobs, and contribute to economic growth—that is, unless the government removes their incentives for doing so.

Remember that the wealthy don't have to make more money. Many of them can live indefinitely on their existing wealth at their current standard of living. And when they exercise their option not to invest, it decreases the job opportunities of less wealthy people who have no choice but to continue working. It's an unfortunate fact of life that in some ways we need the wealthy just as much as they need us—that is, we need them to invest and create jobs, and they need us to work for them.[3]

Instead of lassoing the wealthy with high taxes, we promote economic growth by minimizing the government's burden on investors and entrepreneurs. It's no accident that America began a long period of unprecedented growth in the early 1980s after we dramatically cut top marginal income tax rates. During this time federal tax revenue steadily increased, disproving many dire predictions that lowering tax rates would bankrupt the government. It's also worth recalling that total federal revenue has averaged roughly 18.5 percent of GDP over the last half-century. The precise rate varies from year to year, but the average remained relatively constant both before and after the tax cuts of the early 1980s.

Bottom line: cutting taxes, not raising them, increases government revenues. But politicians have a natural impulse to raise taxes in tough economic times to compensate for declining revenues. Crucially, a balanced budget amendment may strengthen this impulse, as Congress will look for a new revenue stream after deficit spending is eliminated. That's why a well-written balanced budget amendment should make it difficult for Congress to raise tax rates or impose new taxes.

Nevertheless, I would still consider supporting a balanced budget amendment that did not contain that kind of restriction. While congressional liberals may indeed use a balanced budget amendment as an excuse to try to raise taxes, their success is by no means assured due to a simple political reality: tax hikes are almost always deeply unpopular. Any politician or political party that tried to balance the budget by raising taxes would probably not stay in office very long.

The entire debt crisis, in fact, stems in large part from Congress's attempt to surmount popular opposition to tax hikes. A fiscally responsible Congress would not increase spending without increasing taxes to pay for it. Because no one wants to pay higher taxes, politicians face a natural political restraint against voting for higher spending. But Congress gets around this problem by funding new spending through debt rather than through tax hikes. Approving tax hikes would entail an immediate political cost, but the consequences of deficit spending are put off to the future, meaning politicians can increase spending without paying a political price for doing so.

If Congress were required to balance its budget each year, it could not increase spending without either raising taxes or making offsetting spending cuts—and both options would be politically unpopular. In this respect, members could not go on a spending spree without also going on a taxing spree or a budget cutting spree. And if they took either option, it would be at their own political peril.

I'm not arguing that Congress should never increase spending. I'm just saying that members who vote to do so should immediately stand accountable to those who will pay for it—and a balanced budget amendment would enforce that kind of accountability.

★ ★ ★

Realistically, even under the most optimistic scenario it will take several years to get a balanced budget amendment approved. The Founding Fathers deliberately made constitutional amendments difficult to pass: Congress must first propose the amendment by the requisite two-thirds margin in both houses, and then three-fourths of the states must ratify it.

Nevertheless, I believe passing and ratifying a balanced budget amendment is more feasible now than ever before. In the mid-1990s, the U.S. House of Representatives passed a balanced budget amendment by the requisite two-thirds margin, and the Senate came within *one vote* of doing the same (one Republican apparently changed his mind at the last minute). Since then, the national debt has grown by roughly $10 trillion, increasing the urgency of approving this amendment. Meanwhile, the overwhelming majority of state legislatures continue to pass balanced budgets every year (often because their own state constitutions compel them to do so), and would probably find little difficulty requiring Congress to do the same.

Public opinion decisively backs this effort. A May 2011 Sachs/Mason-Dixon poll shows overwhelming public support for a balanced budget amendment, with 65 percent of Americans supporting it and just 27 percent opposed. The amendment was backed by 81 percent of Republicans, 68 percent of independents, and a plurality of Democrats. Notably, by a 46 percent to 21 percent margin, respondents said they would be "more likely" to support a presidential candidate who backed a balanced budget amendment.[4]

We should note that if Congress approved the amendment and it were ratified by the states, it would not take effect immediately; the amendment would likely contain a delayed-implementation clause providing that it would only take force a specified number of years following its ratification.

Unfortunately, these kinds of delayed-implementation provisions seem to be a necessary evil; many members of Congress, even some big supporters of a balanced budget amendment, would not even consider voting for an amendment that would take effect immediately upon ratification. This urge to postpone painful yet necessary reform reminds me of the prayer attributed to Augustine of Hippo (who later became known as St. Augustine): "Grant me chastity and continence, but not yet." While I certainly understand the natural instinct to delay unpleasant tasks, I find it ironic that it is precisely this type of thinking (or lack thereof) that created the debt crisis in the first place.

In any event, since Congress will not be subject to a balanced budget amendment for at least several years, it should fill the gap by immediately enacting spending reform legislation that puts the budget process on a gradual "glide path" to becoming balanced.

The ideal spending reform would closely mirror a balanced budget amendment by requiring Congress to reduce its spending by 1 percent of GDP each year until (a) spending reaches 18 percent of GDP, and (b) federal revenue equals or exceeds federal outlays. It would also require that any exception to these rules, and any effort to raise the debt ceiling, be approved by a supermajority vote in both houses of Congress.

Why, you might ask, shouldn't we just enact this kind statutory spending limitation and dispense altogether with the time-consuming process of amending the Constitution? The answer is simple: unlike a constitutional amendment, a statute can be amended or repealed by a simple-majority vote (assuming there is no presidential veto). And because balancing the budget will inevitably be contentious, Congress would probably not leave a statutory spending cap fully intact for very long.

That is precisely what happened with a previous well-written statutory spending limitation, the so-called Graham-Rudman-Hollings Balanced Budget and Emergency Deficit Control Act of 1985, as amended by the Budget and Emergency Deficit Control Reaffirmation Act of 1987. That legislation mandated automatic spending cuts, known as "sequesters," in the event that the deficit exceeded targets specified by the statute.

If followed, Graham-Rudman-Hollings would have produced a balanced budget. But alas, Congress—unwilling to make difficult choices even when compelled by a law of its own making—effectively repealed the law by enacting the Budget Enforcement Act of 1990. New spending restrictions would inevitably meet the same fate—and sooner rather than later.

That is not to say a statutory spending cap would be useless. Once Congress puts a spending limit in place, it would face intense political pressure to honor that limit for at least a few years—hopefully long enough to get a balanced budget amendment passed and prepare for it to take effect.

★ ★ ★

Any effective federal budget-balancing mechanism—whether statutory, constitutional, or some combination of the two—will restrict the federal government's ability to acquire and spend money, thus diminishing its size and power and enhancing individual freedom. In sum, balancing the budget enhances individual liberty, which in turn increases prosperity.

Think of it this way: when you feed a living organism, it tends to grow larger and stronger. Reduce its food supply, and it becomes smaller and weaker. Governments respond in a similar fashion, and money is their food. And after feeding at an all-day, all-night, all-you-can-eat buffet for decades, the bloated federal government is now crushing our economy.

This dynamic reminds me of something Israeli prime minister Benjamin Netanyahu told me while I was visiting with him in December 2010. After I explained to him my conviction that the most immediate threat to America's peace and prosperity is our national debt, Netanyahu smiled, nodded, and told me a story. He explained that when he was in officer training school, his commanding officer ordered him to compete against two other trainees in a difficult, 50-yard race where each runner had to carry a person on his back.

One of Netanyahu's competitors was a strong, husky guy who had to carry a short, skinny man. His other competitor was short and skinny, but had to carry a big, heavy man. Netanyahu and the man he was assigned to carry were both of roughly the same build.

Predictably, the husky trainee with the skinny passenger won the race. Netanyahu finished second, while the skinny guy carrying the heavy passenger collapsed after a few steps and could not finish the contest.

Netanyahu then drew an analogy that was at once refreshingly simple and surprisingly profound. He explained that each runner was like a national economy, and each passenger was like a government. The economy in each country is required to "carry" the government. If the economy is strong and the government is small, then the former will have relatively little difficulty carrying the latter, like the big runner with the skinny passenger. If, on the other hand, the government is too "heavy" for the economy to bear, then it wears down the economy, as the husky passenger did to the smaller runner.

In that last scenario, Netanyahu continued, the only solution is to put the government on a strict diet while simultaneously strengthening the economy. As the economy grows stronger and the government becomes leaner, the team becomes more effective.

This analogy holds some useful insights for our effort to balance the budget. If the U.S. government has grown so big that even the largest, most robust economy in world history is struggling under its weight, and if the government is continuing to grow faster than the economy, then our overall task is crystal clear: we have to shrink the government and strengthen the economy.

We need to put the federal government on a diet by restricting its source of food: money. Just as a limitless supply of money has enabled the federal government to expand its size, scope, cost, and reach—all but shattering the notion that it is supposed to wield only enumerated powers—limiting its money supply will force it to focus on those things that it is uniquely authorized and empowered to do.

The time has arrived to break the vicious cycle of soft tyranny. But politicians won't make the change on their own; the voters have to demand it. Americans need to send them an unambiguous message: either steadfastly support a balanced budget amendment—and back other structural spending reforms that will facilitate the move to a balanced budget—or in the next election you will be replaced by someone who will.

PART III

How Restoring Constitutionally Limited Government Will Help Balance the Budget

★ ★ ★

CHAPTER SIX

Achieving Fiscal Balance through Federalism

During the 150-year period in which America generally adhered to principles of federalism, members of Congress understood that not every evil in the world can or should be solved by the federal government. In other words, they respected the concept of constitutionally limited government.

Within that time frame, the federal government was a lot more affordable than it is today. This disparity cannot be explained by inflation, westward expansion, a rapidly growing population, increasing threats to American national security, or any factor other than the unfettered expansion of the size and reach of the federal government.

Since the Great Depression, the federal government has been operating without any substantive limits on the scope of its authority, resorting to deficit spending and exploding our national debt to the point that the American people can no longer afford the government itself.

In order to make the federal government affordable again, we need to restore constitutionally limited government. As we undertake that process, we have to remember that limited government used to be the norm in America. Only as it ceased to be the norm did federal spending escalate significantly. There is a direct connection between these two trends of expanding government and unsustainable spending. By limiting the former, we help to eliminate the latter.

★ ★ ★

Before the Great Depression, the federal government consistently operated on a budget ranging between 1.5 percent and 4 percent of annual GDP, with the percentage usually at the lower end of that range.[1] There were only two significant exceptions: the ratio shot up briefly to about 13 percent during the Civil War and to about 24 percent during World War I. After each of those wars ended, spending levels returned largely to normal levels within a few years.[2]

Things changed dramatically during the New Deal era. In the mid-1930s we crossed the 10 percent barrier for the first time during peacetime, and since 1940 the federal spending-to-GDP ratio has never dropped back below that threshold. Due to World War II, the ratio reached its all-time peak of almost

48 percent in 1945, then dropped down to about 13 percent by 1948. The figure increased briefly to around 21 percent during the Korean War, hovered at 17–19.5 percent from 1955 through 1974, and remained at 20–23 percent for the following two decades. In 1996, it dipped below 20 percent and remained there until 2008.

The ratio has jumped in the last few years, hitting 24.9 percent in 2009, 23.82 percent in 2010, and 25.3 percent in 2011, that last figure marking the first time since World War II and its immediate aftermath that the ratio has exceeded 25 percent. In essence, this means for every dollar moving through the U.S. economy in 2011, more than a quarter is consumed by the federal government.[3]

This spending expands the reach and increases the intrusiveness of government, eroding Americans' freedom. Congress is increasingly funding this spending spree through deficit spending, but it is also enabled by excessively high tax rates. In collecting these burdensome taxes, Congress arrogantly assumes it knows how to use our precious time and money more wisely than we do.

That does not mean *any* tax burden is intolerable. Some government is essential, and it needs tax revenue to perform its necessary functions. Although there is no universal standard for identifying when a tax burden becomes excessive, it is a self-evident injustice when taxpayers, whether some of them or all, have to labor many months out of every year just to pay their taxes. Worse still, during their months of federal servitude, taxpayers are working to fund an unnecessarily complex and demanding labyrinth of federal laws, regulations, and bureaucratic hurdles that inhibit their ability to conduct business and earn the very money the government is confiscating.

In fairness, a large portion of our federal tax revenue is put to good use. America, and the world in general, is a better, safer place thanks to numerous indispensible services provided by the federal government and funded by tax revenue. But that still doesn't justify our current tax burden.

High taxes, deficit spending, and the rising national debt are all symptoms of the same core problem: the federal government's assumption of too many responsibilities. This trend stems in part from the widespread assumption that because the federal government controls vast resources, there are few problems it cannot solve.

That assumption is both dangerous and incorrect. The federal government is neither omniscient nor omnipotent. It is operated by imperfect, mortal beings who make mistakes and are subject to many limitations, just like anybody else. Our faith properly belongs with God, not with the government.

Of course, the government can accomplish certain "big" tasks—for example, providing for our national defense—better than any other institution. But its ability to accomplish *some* tasks can create the false impression that it can accomplish *any* task.

Politicians are programmed to say "yes" to spending. They need a mechanism to help them say "no." A balanced budget amendment would do precisely that.

But even before that amendment is ratified, we need a framework through which taxpayers and members of Congress can confidently, thoughtfully, and respectfully evaluate what the federal government does with our time and money. This framework would assist Congress in identifying instances where it is overstepping its bounds and carelessly spending our hard-earned money.

As we develop this framework, remember that some people are perfectly happy with big government. They will naturally want our standard of review for federal spending programs to be as broad and permissive as possible, approving any expenditure that "does good things" and isn't obviously wasteful or duplicative. However, as this book has shown, that is a woefully inadequate standard that can eventually lead to tyranny.

Doing something good and avoiding waste should be *preconditions* to approving or continuing a federal program. Once those preconditions have been met, a program should be evaluated according to the three basic criteria outlined below. Scrutinizing federal programs in this way will promote the cause of constitutionally limited government and make balancing the budget a more manageable task until we ratify a balanced-budget amendment.

Is the Program Better Left to Civil Society?

First, the federal government should focus on governing. There are a number of functions that can be performed *only* by government, such as enacting civil and criminal laws, adjudicating guilt or innocence, punishing crime, providing for national defense, levying taxes, and regulating trade. A free society is well served by a government that resists the temptation to expand this list, leaving broader attempts to "do good things" to civil society—that is, families, individuals, religious institutions, non-profit foundations, and other non-governmental entities.

The question is not whether we should do good things; it is whether the coercive power of government will be reserved, as it should be, for tasks that no other institution can perform. Asking this question about every federal program will help us to end the relentless expansion of government power, while leaving the government more time and resources for fulfilling its proper, limited responsibilities in a competent way that respects individual liberty.

Is the Program Better Left to State and Local Government?

Even when a program is clearly within the rightful scope of government, we must ask whether it falls within the constitutionally enumerated powers of the federal government, or within the broad, undefined powers of state governments.

Each of America's fifty state governments is sovereign within its own sphere of authority and is not a mere political subdivision of a single, national sovereign. Given that the most basic purpose of government is to maintain order and prevent anarchy, the federal government should go to great lengths to prevent the kind of conflict and confusion that emerges when one sovereign government steps on another's domain.

Because Congress, unlike the states, is vastly exceeding its authority today, it is Congress's powers that must be curtailed. Otherwise the distinction between federal and state power will continue to fade, risking a dangerous clash between the federal government and aggrieved state representatives.

To determine whether a federal program or proposed program should instead be left to the states, we should ask whether it would have fallen within the federal government's power before the New Deal. Constitutional amendments, technological advances, and other historic developments must, of course, be taken into account, just as competing interpretive approaches should be considered on their own merits.

The precise interpretive methodology is relatively unimportant as long as the discussion focuses on the text and founding-era understanding of the Constitution and, most important, the Constitution's basic premise that the powers of the federal government are few and defined, while those of the states are numerous and indefinite.

Will Eliminating the Program Cause Avoidable Suffering?

Finally, although the first two criteria may suggest that many federal programs should be eliminated, that determination must be tempered by practical, humanitarian considerations.

Congress should carefully consider how the elimination of any federal program might impact vulnerable Americans who rely on it. When Congress decides to discontinue such a program, it should, wherever possible, phase in that change gradually in order to ease the burden on the program's beneficiaries. That transition period would also give state governments, local governments, and civil society an opportunity to make arrangements to fill the resulting void.

Obviously, Congress should not perpetuate programs that plainly exceed constitutional limitations on federal power, especially unmanageable programs that are threatening to bankrupt the country. However, having made millions of Americans reliant on federal largess, Congress is morally obligated to eliminate those benefits in a measured, humane way that minimizes hardships on American citizens.

If Congress identifies a constitutionally defective program whose elimination would cause severe, widespread hardship, it should consider ways to reduce or otherwise change the program to make it constitutionally compliant. If that proves impossible, Congress can gain legitimate authority over the program by proposing a constitutional amendment. However, a constitutional amendment to *expand* federal power is potentially dangerous, and should be drafted narrowly enough to clarify that Congress's authority remains strictly limited.

In sum, Congress has long been content with evaluating federal programs on the basis of whether they accomplish good things and do not waste money. Congress needs to recognize that these are only preliminary questions, and that each program should be evaluated based on the criteria detailed above. If the program deals with a uniquely governmental function and falls within the federal government's enumerated powers, it can be approved or continued, subject to ongoing inquiries into its effectiveness and cost-efficiency. Whenever a program fails to meet those conditions, Congress should consider downsizing or eliminating it, taking into account whether such a step would severely affect vulnerable populations. If cutting a program would cause suffering, it should either be phased out gradually or reformed to make it compatible with the Constitution.

★ ★ ★

Most federal programs subjected to this three-part analysis will fit into one of three categories:

(1) Government operations that would have been considered federal responsibilities prior to the New Deal era—including the realms of the military, immigration, patents and trademarks, aviation, and federal courts—and that:

(a) have a close nexus to a federal power enumerated in the Constitution

(b) could not be performed effectively by the states, and

(c) are necessary to maintain peace, order, and security throughout America.

(2) Government operations that would *not* have been considered federal responsibilities prior to the New Deal era—including those involving the regulation of intrastate activities like labor, manufacturing, agriculture, mining, and education—and that:

(a) historically were performed by the states

(b) are sometimes performed by the states, creating some redundancies, and

(c) could in many instances be performed effectively by the states without federal involvement.

(3) Entitlements and other household-assistance programs that would *not* have been considered federal responsibilities prior to the New Deal era—including Social Security, Medicare, Medicaid, Supplemental Nutrition Assistance (food stamps), federal housing assistance, and federal unemployment insurance—and that:

(a) are distinct from the basic operations of government in that their purpose is not to regulate or protect, but to redistribute wealth in hopes of easing the burden of the poor, the elderly, and other vulnerable Americans, and

(b) could in many instances be provided effectively by the states and by private entities without federal involvement.

Let's take a quick look at each of these categories in turn.

Category One

The line between categories one and two can be difficult to discern—partly because the defining criteria are subject to some debate, and partly because most federal agencies perform functions in both categories. It is nonetheless safe to say that most of the roughly $1.8 trillion spent annually between these two categories is devoted to category one. In fact, well over $1 trillion is spent just on national defense (including veterans benefits) and interest on the national debt, both of which fit easily into category one.

Category one expenditures are devoted to endeavors that play an essential, constitutionally sanctioned role in maintaining law, order, and security. Although Americans might not always agree on precisely how much money should be devoted to such efforts or exactly how it should be spent, most would agree that it is both acceptable and necessary for the federal government to perform these constitutionally assigned duties.

The federal government is, by its size and bureaucratic nature, often highly inefficient. Therefore, Congress should never become so complacent with category one programs that it fails to monitor them carefully and weed out inefficiencies. But category one spending is easy to defend because these programs are clearly sanctioned by the Constitution, involve functions that can be provided only by government, and could not be provided effectively on a state-by-state basis.

It's hard to imagine the federal government engaging in perpetual deficit spending and running up an astronomical level of debt if it focused solely on these programs—the $2.2 trillion the federal government collects annually is more than enough to cover all category one spending.

Category Two

Category two programs are more difficult to defend than those in category one. Although they are, by nature, governmental activities, category two programs lack the close nexus to an enumerated power found in category one programs.

It's difficult to say just how much money Congress spends each year on category two programs, given that most federal departments operate both in category one and in category two, and there is no way to discern from their budgets how much money is spent in each category. But given that the federal government takes in around $2.2 trillion in annual revenues and spends $1.8 trillion on category one and category two programs combined, Congress could, using current revenue, still balance its budget each year while fully funding both category one and category two.

Category Three

Programs in category three collectively receive about $2 trillion per year, representing *well over half* of annual federal outlays. The figure is roughly equivalent to the amount of money the federal government currently collects each year in tax and other revenue.[4]

These programs are most difficult to justify or to reconcile with the text and original understanding of the Constitution. It is hard to see, by any stretch of the imagination, how one could argue that these kinds of assistance and entitlement programs can be provided only—or even most efficiently—by the federal government.

Don't get me wrong; caring for the poor, sick, elderly, and unemployed is both laudable and necessary. I wouldn't want to live in a society that failed to meet the basic needs of its most vulnerable members. Nevertheless, we should not assume that pervasive suffering would ensue if the federal government gradually divested itself of that role.

Large, government-funded social programs tend to "crowd out" charitable giving—partly because they necessitate high tax rates that leave would-be donors with less money to give, and partly because they create the (often incorrect) impression that the government will always address the needs of the poor. In this respect, a move toward constitutionally limited government will promote the welfare of vulnerable populations by enlisting the invaluable assistance of churches, charities, neighborhood organizations, families, and other elements of civil society. The combined efforts and resources of all these groups could form a far more effective societal safety net than bureaucratic government programs ever could.

In any event, if constitutionally limited government were restored to America, each state would have the opportunity to assess the distinct needs of its own population, taking into account not only the capacity of civil society, but also the costs, benefits, tax implications, and overall societal impact of each of its programs. Competition among the diverse states would result in continual innovations and improvements in the delivery of services.

Throughout America's history, services for the sick, aged, and other vulnerable populations have been—and in many instances still are—provided by civil society, states, and local governments without any funding or other involvement by the federal government. A complete, immediate federal withdrawal from this role would surely cause immense problems. But if managed carefully and phased in over time, such a withdrawal could be accomplished without severe disruption, as states and civil society assume federal duties that they are more competent to fulfill.

★ ★ ★

America has always been a compassionate nation, and we always will be. And it is *because* of our compassion, not in spite of it, that we need to stop Congress from overextending itself and mortgaging the future of every American man, woman, and child through its unsustainable spending.

The American people provide Congress with a significant part of their earnings every year, but that's still not enough to cover what Congress spends. As a result, long-standing programs that Congress has promised to fund in perpetuity, and that have fostered dependence among millions of Americans, are now in a precarious position. As we move toward a full-blown debt crisis, each of those programs face a growing risk of undergoing immediate, drastic cuts that would inevitably cause prolonged suffering.

If we really care about the most vulnerable among us—those who are most dependent on the same federal programs that are driving the federal government deeply into debt—then we will insist that Congress immediately begin to restore constitutionally limited government, both as an end in itself and as a means toward achieving a balanced budget. Should we fail to take this critical step now, perhaps because we want to *appear* generous and compassionate, we will not be defending the poor; we'll just be guaranteeing a future in which they will bear the brunt of the draconian spending cuts that will result from our nation's fiscal insolvency.

To whatever degree we succeed in restoring constitutionally limited government, it will make it easier for Congress to balance its budget while funding those programs that we, as a nation, believe are the most vital. That, in turn, will promote economic growth that, consistent with every economic boom in American history, will foster more charitable giving and will leave state and local governments with more flexibility to fund programs previously administered at the federal level.

Everyone benefits when the federal government operates within its assigned sphere. By the same token, everyone will ultimately be harmed when the federal government operates without any meaningful restraint.

CHAPTER SEVEN

★ ★ ★

Restraining the Federal Regulatory Monster

In exceeding its enumerated powers, Congress causes major fiscal and constitutional problems by doing things it should *not* do. There are, however, problems that arise when Congress fails to do what it *should* be doing.

For example, Congress habitually delegates much of its lawmaking power to executive-branch agencies, thereby avoiding accountability and creating a legal system that hinders economic growth. These laws, adopted by unelected and unaccountable bureaucrats, are often poorly designed and arbitrarily enforced, resulting in lost jobs and depressed investment.

A government that makes lawmakers accountable to the people at regular intervals is far more likely to promote—or at least, not to depress—economic growth than is a government that insulates lawmakers from the political process. That's because investors and entrepreneurs will take the risks necessary to create jobs only when they are reasonably confident the government won't arbitrarily interfere with their ability to earn a living. A transparent, accountable government earns the trust of job creators, while the same can't be said for a government in which politically insulated functionaries make laws in the shadows.

If Congress were to reclaim its constitutional lawmaking responsibilities, the whole federal government would become more accountable to the people and more conducive to economic growth. Such growth would in turn generate additional tax revenue, making it easier for Congress to balance its budget.

★ ★ ★

Article I, Section 1 of the Constitution provides that "[a]ll legislative powers herein granted shall be vested in a Congress of the United States, which shall consist of a Senate and House of Representatives." Legislative power is, of course, the power to make generally applicable, enforceable rules carrying the force of law. And although the Constitution vests that power in Congress, rules carrying the force of law are routinely drafted, promulgated, implemented, and enforced today entirely within executive branch agencies. Bafflingly, Congress itself has promoted this practice.

This decades-long trend might appear innocuous; after all, some may reason, administrative agencies have valuable expertise that uniquely qualifies them to adopt rules and regulations in their respective domains. Since those agencies are funded by and remain subject to the supervision of Congress, why should we worry about them usurping Congress's legislative role?

The problem with this trend is that it helps politicians avoid accountability. Because oppressive, arbitrary, and unduly burdensome laws are generally unpopular, in a representative government those responsible for such laws normally have two choices: fix or repeal the laws, or do nothing and risk losing the next election. Naturally, most elected officials choose the first option. But when these laws have been effectively approved by unelected bureaucrats, the laws' authors face no democratic pressure to reform or abolish them because no one knows who these people are. Thus, these laws tend to persist for a long time despite their well-deserved unpopularity.

The founding generation designed our republic so that lawmakers would be held accountable to the American people through regular elections. But that system is decaying as executive agencies acquire more and more power to legislate by administrative fiat.

Defenders of this practice deny that it violates the principles of representative government, arguing that executive agencies (a) answer to the elected president, and (b) wield only such power as Congress, by law, chooses to give them.

Let's address the former argument first. With good reason, the Constitution doesn't entrust the task of federal lawmaking to a single, elected chief executive; it divides that power among two houses of Congress and renders that power subject to presidential veto. This system incorporates 536 elected officials today. The founding generation deliberately dispersed lawmaking power widely, understanding—as most of us still understand—that vesting legislative authority in one person, even an elected official, constitutes a dangerous centralization of power.

It follows *a fortiori* that we can't vest legislative power in a group of *non*-elected bureaucrats simply because, in one way or another, they work for an elected chief executive. Most of the administrative officials who make and enforce regulations carrying the force of law are neither hired by the president nor subject to termination by him, and are therefore largely insulated from the electoral process.

Each department and agency is generally "headed" by a presidential appointee who must be confirmed by the Senate and serves "subject to the pleasure of the President"—that is, the president can fire the appointee at any time, for any reason or for no reason at all. But most of the top officials who run the agencies' day-to-day operations are career-track employees who, by law, cannot be removed for political reasons. While that kind of "non-political" system might sound nice, what it really means is that many of those who now make laws are, by law, protected from the will of the people who are governed by those laws.

Without question, there are many hard-working men and women who serve in our executive agencies. My point is simply that, unlike the president and members of Congress, bureaucrats aren't subject to elections and therefore should not be entrusted with lawmaking power.

The second argument—that executive agencies exercise only such lawmaking power as Congress by law chooses to delegate— is similarly flawed. It is, of course, true that every member of Congress is elected; it is likewise true that executive agencies may not promulgate regulations carrying the force of law without authority from Congress. Nevertheless, members of Congress have been much too permissive in ceding their law-making responsibilities to non-elected bureaucrats and have failed to vigilantly oversee the exercise of that authority.

This trend seems puzzling, but there's a reason for it: by delegating their authority, members of Congress gain something they want and lose something they don't want. If, for example, a member of Congress wants federal restrictions on greenhouse gas emissions but does not want to answer to angry constituents who oppose those regulations, lawmaking by administrative fiat might provide an attractive course of action.

A member of Congress facing that dilemma might well encourage, or at least allow, the Environmental Protection Agency to take action under the Clean Air Act, which essentially empowers the EPA to propose, promulgate, and enforce regulations to give us clean air. This, to be sure, oversimplifies the Clean Air Act, but it illustrates the point that Congress sometimes legislates using broad, unobjectionable terminology. Executive agencies then have to "fill in the gaps" by decreeing and enforcing the actual regulations that Congress itself failed to define.

In the scenario above, when the EPA eventually promulgates restrictions on greenhouse gas emissions, supportive members of Congress will have the perfect answer for angry constituents who oppose the action: "I'm not responsible for the EPA's actions. I didn't write or vote for these regulations; I voted only for clean air. If you don't like the way the EPA has exercised its statutory authority to promote clean air, you'll have to complain to the EPA."

This dismissive, craven method of legislating removes the type of accountability that is the lifeblood of any properly functioning representative government. It also disrupts economic growth, as the opaque, arbitrary regulatory regime creates uncertainty and makes would-be investors reluctant to invest their money and create jobs.

While Congress deserves a large share of the blame for abdicating its responsibilities, the executive agencies themselves are not without fault. Even when the process of passing a regulation is more transparent, it is often still deeply flawed. For instance, the EPA sometimes invites concerned citizens to submit formal comments during the public "notice and comment" period of the rulemaking process. That process, however, simply cloaks a manifestly undemocratic process behind a thin veneer of legislative legitimacy.

While "notice and comment" might appear to be a participatory process—perhaps faintly resembling public hearings conducted by elected legislators—appearances can be deceiving, and in this context they are. Public comments might occasionally result in marginal changes to a proposed regulatory regime, but they rarely alter the basic policy objectives of the proposed regulations. And even in those rare instances when public comments do change an agency's proposed course of action, the changes more closely reflect the demands of the agency's most vocal and well-funded critics than they do the will of the people as expressed through the ballot box. This is not a recipe for good government.

Additionally, the EPA and other regulatory agencies might defend their conduct by noting that anyone who believes they are exceeding their authority can take them to court. However, in most lawsuits challenging an administrative regulation, courts defer to the issuing agency, reasoning that it has broad discretion to decide how best to pursue its statutory mandate from Congress.

Thus, when a citizen opposes an administrative regulation promulgated by an executive agency, he will be hard-pressed to gain an audience with any public official who is willing to hold himself accountable to the public. This is not how our republican government was intended to operate—and it cannot continue to govern like this if we hope to maintain our customary levels of economic growth. Our ability to create and retain jobs, and even Congress's ability to balance its budget, will remain tenuous as long as elected, accountable members of Congress continue to transfer their lawmaking power to unelected, unaccountable, executive branch bureaucrats.

★ ★ ★

Fortunately, there is a solution. Congress needs to enact legislation that would permanently sunset administrative regulations after a finite period of time—ideally no more than six months—unless Congress enacted those specific regulations into law (subject, of course, to presidential approval or veto). That approach would re-insert elected officials into the legislative equation, ensuring public accountability for the sensitive task of lawmaking. As members of Congress considered new regulatory initiatives, they would inevitably hear from concerned citizens—both those favoring and those opposing each set of regulations—and would understand that, if they chose to ignore public sentiment, they could be held accountable at the next election.

Like all efforts to make government more accountable to the governed, any push for this kind of reform will draw considerable criticism. Many of the critics will be those who benefit—financially or otherwise—from the current system, and they will argue that any departure from the status quo would be disruptive or even dangerous. Critics tend to raise some variation of this argument in response to almost *any* effort to transfer lawmaking power from the unelected to the elected. Whether faced with an all-powerful despot or a well-intentioned, idealistic bureaucrat, those who value liberty will recognize the self-serving nature of these objections, knowing that the most loyal supporters of any form of despotism are those who personally benefit from it.

Other critics, while perhaps not benefiting directly from the status quo, might be influenced by the commonly held but mistaken belief that governments function best when critical policy decisions are made by institutional, career-track officials—highly specialized experts whose judgment, wisdom, and experience are so valuable that they must be insulated from the unpredictable electoral process.[1] The unwashed masses of voters and elected officials, the argument goes, have no such expertise, often fail to "see the big picture," and inexplicably tend to change their policy preferences from time to time.

This argument suffers from three fundamental flaws. First, this reasoning is incompatible with the republican form of government established by the Constitution. Under that document, legislative power is vested in an elected Congress—even though *no one* elected to that or any other legislative body could ever claim to be a subject-matter expert in every area in which he or she legislates. While expertise and consistency may be good things to have in government (and can be taken into account by voters), they are not nearly as important as is accountability. And accountability cannot exist when legislative power is vested in individuals who, however smart or well-intentioned, are not subject to elections.

Second, taken to its logical conclusion, the "trust the experts" argument would, however incrementally, erode representative government and transform our republic into a technocratic oligarchy—a government run not by popularly elected representatives, but by an elite group of highly disciplined, specialized experts. Such a government may operate efficiently, but it could not be trusted to respect life, liberty, and property any more than a garden-variety dictator could. And while the trains might well run on time in a technocratic oligarchy, the world has learned through bitter experience that the most effective and efficient governments are often the most dangerous. We should be wary of creating such a system, even if only by degrees.

Third, the most significant benefits associated with administrative bureaucracies could easily be preserved in a system in which Congress itself had to approve regulations. It may well be true that government regulators have unique expertise in their specific area or industry, and in this system they would still be free to propose new rules to Congress, which could benefit from their insight while retaining the final say on approving or rejecting their recommendations. Thus, America would stand to lose little and gain much by treating administratively promulgated regulatory regimes as proposals rather than enacted laws.

★ ★ ★

As lawmaking power is returned to officials who are accountable to the people, our laws will become more respectful of the people's rights to life, liberty, and property. This will in turn promote economic growth, as investors and other job creators become more active once they discover that the power to make law—and with it the power to regulate almost any business enterprise out of existence—is no longer entrusted to unaccountable, unelected, and unknown bureaucrats.

Members of Congress want to keep their jobs, and they understand they will not remain in office for long if the laws they create thwart job creation. Consequently, as long as the people can see what they're doing and hold them accountable, members of Congress have a built-in incentive to pass pro-market, pro-growth laws.

For that reason, our elected lawmakers should guard jealously the legislative power granted them by the Constitution. Taking this important step toward restoring constitutionally limited government will promote sustained economic growth. And that growth will increase federal tax revenues, making it easier for Congress to forego deficit spending and balance its budget.

★ ★ ★

From Boston to Philadelphia

In December 1773, a group of merchants in Boston boarded an English trading ship and threw imported crates of tea into Boston Harbor. Applauded by some and condemned by others, this defiant act was a protest against what American colonists increasingly viewed as an overreaching national government that imposed excessive taxes on nearly everything, including staples such as sugar, tobacco, and tea. After nearly two centuries living under the English crown, the colonists had learned that their London-based national government was as quick to tax and regulate as it was slow to respect local self-rule.

To make matters worse, while their taxes steadily enriched the king, the colonists had no representation in the British Parliament.

Unlike landowners producing wool in Kent or shopkeepers selling textiles in Devonshire, colonial Americans had no say over the increasingly intrusive and unjust policies that governed their daily lives. In their eyes, the British crown had become unresponsive, distant, oppressive, and greedy.

Through the Boston Tea Party and other demonstrations of civil (and not-so-civil) disobedience, the colonists sent a message across the Atlantic. The message reached London, but it was also heard across the rivers of New England, in the tobacco fields of Virginia, and within every backwater village of the still-fledgling American frontier. This mantra, later memorialized by Benjamin Franklin, is proclaimed today by activists for limited-government: DON'T TREAD ON ME.

It had taken decades for the colonists to conclude that what they *did not* want from their national government exceeded what they *did* want. Paying taxes to London meant that the crown would continue to provide the colonies with the kind of protection and stability that only a world superpower could credibly offer. However, it was dangerous merely to suggest that taxation without representation and myriad other abuses had become too high a price to pay for the king's protection. While increasingly prosperous, colonial America could fairly be compared to a muscular teenager—confident and strong, though still unproven in its ability to survive on its own. But when it finally secured its independence, the budding republic showed maturity and capacity beyond its years.

In hindsight, what made the Boston Tea Party effective was the fact that the economic reality of independence had set in long before colonial Americans fully embraced the philosophical argument for self-government. The act of tossing tea into the sea was a pre-revolutionary outburst that helped to define the quintessentially American concepts of freedom, liberty, local self-government, and individualism. In Boston, a group of Americans rose up and began to cut their historical ties to a centralized, national power that had slid into tyranny.

The risk-to-benefit ratio was grossly stacked against the rebellious colonists. But with the Boston Tea Party, America initiated its struggle for economic freedom. The fledgling nation was not yet a political threat to the stability of the British Empire, but it was a newcomer making waves in the otherwise calm harbors of European traditionalism. These waves would soon morph into devastating tsunamis, as economic grievances against the British crown swelled into political grievances that produced a national fervor for freedom.

While the original call for economic freedom rang from Boston, its political dimension wasn't fully defined until 1787, when the Constitution was drafted in Philadelphia. Thus, it took us fourteen years to get from Boston, where American protestors expressed what they did *not* want from their national government, to Philadelphia, where our Founding Fathers explained what they *did* want. During these years, Americans fought and won the Revolutionary War, organized a national government under the Articles of Confederation, and then agreed on a new model of government to correct the flaws of the previous one.

Fortunately, we Americans today don't need fourteen years to get from "Boston," where we explain the inadequacies our federal government, to "Philadelphia," where we stipulate how to reform that government. We don't need to fight a war, overthrow the oppressive regime of a king, or fashion a new system of government. The answers we need today are essentially the same as they were in Philadelphia during the summer of 1787.

As our Constitution still provides, what we need is a *limited-purpose* national government. It should be empowered to perform just a few basic tasks—provide for national defense, regulate interstate and international trade, establish a uniform system of weights and measures, regulate immigration, protect trademarks, copyrights, and patents, and fulfill some other specific responsibilities—while leaving all other powers to the states. And though we have amended the Constitution from time to time, the document's core purpose remains the same as it was in 1787: to protect the people against the perils of a large, powerful, national government, which by nature tends to relentlessly expand its authority and demand more money from its citizens as it does so.

We don't have to re-invent the wheel. If we will once again use the Constitution as a mechanism for guiding robust political debate about the proper role of the federal government, we will find that the Founding Fathers largely struck the proper balance between state power and federal power. Finding and restoring that balance is essential to maintaining freedom and restoring prosperity in America.

★ ★ ★

As I have argued throughout this book, we can accelerate the restoration of limited government by amending the Constitution to restrict Congress's authority to borrow. A balanced budget amendment will produce synergies that we desperately need. Restricting Congress's power to engage in perpetual deficit spending will lead us to constitutionally limited government; and focusing on constitutionally limited government will help Congress abandon its perpetual deficit spending.

The time has come once again for Americans to progress from Boston to Philadelphia. And the fastest way to transition from protesting what we *don't* want to articulating what we *do* want is to support the twin causes of constitutionally limited government and a balanced budget amendment. Americans who love freedom and want the prosperity it brings should seek out and support political candidates who will champion these causes.

The establishment today regards the push for constitutionally limited government as neither understandable nor reasonable, much like the British regarded the Boston Tea Party. But joining a movement to halt the excesses of a large, powerful national government is at once reflective, corrective, and deeply rooted in American individualism. It is a spontaneous reaction to a dangerous threat, like an immune system responding to an infectious agent or parasite.

There is an upsurge in conservative activism today aiming to restore limited government. Supporters of this movement view our nation as strong, but in a weakened condition, infected by the disease of a national debt approaching $15 trillion. Just like the colonial rebellion, this movement is more than a response to any single government abuse; it is an awakening, an instinctive reaction for national self-preservation. It is a grassroots, locally organized effort that extends nationwide. It is driven not by an external leader, but by an internal realization that the good of the nation is not well-served by casual participation in the public affairs of this country.

Standing at the forefront of this movement is a new iteration of an old American tradition: the tea party. In all fifty states today, the tea party is spreading the message that the established way of doing business in Washington will no longer suffice. The movement is based on the American ideal that peaceful popular forces can change Washington's internal status quo. Its essence was stated succinctly on a tea partier's t-shirt I recently saw. Responding to some of the most blatantly inaccurate and malicious efforts to marginalize this movement, the t-shirt simply read, "Not an extremist. Not a racist. I am simply no longer silent."

Like our Founding Fathers in the early 1770s, Americans today stand at an historical crossroads. Facing a looming fiscal and economic crisis, we have a short window to decide whether we will adopt painful reforms in the short-term to stave off catastrophe further down the road. While conservatism by its nature implies caution and circumspection, the time has come for bold actions to preserve our nation and our way of life. In the wake of recent government-funded bailouts, staggering stimulus spending, moves toward socialized healthcare, increases in national regulation, and the steady erosion of state sovereignty, we must advance with fearless clarity and conviction the conservative program of limited government.

Government "of the people, by the people, for the people" is made possible through self-motivation and self-sacrifice. That understanding was the rocket-fuel that propelled my candidacy for the U.S. Senate in Utah. My campaign was, at least initially, staffed on every level by volunteers. Funds were often raised only hours before they were needed. Groups of as few as ten and as many as fifty gathered in homes, libraries, parking lots, and at schools to spread our message. Committed activists filled local precinct caucuses, made phone calls, raised funds, and attended rallies because they believed, like I do, in our essential need to restore constitutionally limited government.

The media, with good reason, has characterized my election as a tea party victory. Some predict this type of conservative, grassroots mobilization, which was not entirely unique in 2010, will become far more common in future election cycles. Others have dismissed the trend as a short-lived anomaly in which a few limited-government Davids, by some lucky twist of fate, ousted establishment Goliaths. With a crucial election on the horizon in 2012, the American people will soon prove one of these arguments correct.

The modern-day cargo ship has left its port laden with heavily taxed, government-subsidized goods delivered at a high price to every hard-working American. We have until now been all too willing to pay that price. But a group of over-burdened, over-regulated Americans have once again gathered at the harbor.

How will this confrontation play out? Will the message of these Americans, like that of their predecessors, ultimately lower taxes, give government back to the people, overturn seats of power, and sacrifice national largess in favor of local control? If history is the fortune teller we deem it to be, then our nation's future can be seen in the tea leaves of Boston.

Conclusion

O ur path to national self-preservation lies in the comple-
mentary objectives of restoring constitutionally limited
government and requiring Congress to balance its budget. To
the extent we accomplish those tasks, we will succeed in preserving freedom. To the extent we fail, we will leave to our children
and grandchildren a future clouded by debt, economic stagna-
tion, and an increasingly intrusive and oppressive government.

I ran for the U.S. Senate because I believe we can succeed.
My optimism is encouraged by the growing number of Americans—old and young, black and white, conservative and liberal—who are convinced Congress cannot continue year after
year to spend money that it does not have. More than at any

point in my lifetime, Americans are speaking out for limited government and fiscal responsibility, expressing their demands through civic activism, and making these issues their deciding factor at the ballot box.

My hope is that you count yourself among this growing movement. As I argued at the beginning of this book, regardless of whether you are most concerned about preserving America's entitlement programs, strengthening the economy, or improving America's national defense capabilities, you should support the effort to force accountability, fiscal responsibility, and constitutional limits upon Congress. After all, the federal government's reckless deficit spending threatens the solvency of every government program.

A balanced budget amendment and constitutionally limited government are more than just noble ideals; they are realistic goals. We have both the Constitution and popular opinion on our side. We just have to voice our demands loud enough through the political process that Congress is left with no choice but to accede. In the course of more than two centuries of American history, we have overcome far more daunting challenges. And we can overcome this one.

We can, we must, and we will.

PART IV

★ ★ ★

Four Essential Documents

★ ★ ★

The Articles of Confederation

Agreed to by Congress November 15, 1777; ratified and in force, March 1, 1781.

Preamble

To all to whom these Presents shall come, we, the undersigned, Delegates of the States affixed to our Names, send greeting: Whereas the Delegates of the United States of America in Congress assembled, did on the fifteenth day of November, in the year of our Lord one thousand seven hundred and seventy seven, and in the second year of the Independence of America, agree to certain articles of Confederation and perpetual Union between the states of New Hampshire, Massachusetts-bay,

Rhode Island and Providence Plantations, Connecticut, New York, New Jersey, Pennsylvania, Delaware, Maryland, Virginia, North Carolina, South Carolina, and Georgia, in the words following, viz. Articles of Confederation and perpetual Union between the States of New Hampshire, Massachusetts-bay, Rhode Island and Providence Plantations, Connecticut, New York, New Jersey, Pennsylvania, Delaware, Maryland, Virginia, North Carolina, South Carolina, and Georgia.

Article I. The stile of this confederacy shall be, "The United States of America."

Article II. Each State retains its sovereignty, freedom, and independence, and every power, jurisdiction, and right, which is not by this confederation, expressly delegated to the United States, in Congress assembled.

Article III. The said States hereby severally enter into a firm league of friendship with each other, for their common defence, the security of their liberties, and their mutual and general welfare, binding themselves to assist each other against all force offered to, or attacks made upon them, or any of them, on account of religion, sovereignty, trade, or any other pretence whatever.

Article IV. The better to secure and perpetuate mutual friendship and intercourse among the people of the different States in this union, the free inhabitants of each of these States, paupers, vagabonds, and fugitives from justice excepted, shall be entitled to all privileges and immunities of free citizens in the several States; and the people of each State shall have free ingress and regress to and from any other State, and shall enjoy therein all the privileges of trade and commerce, subject to the same duties, impositions, and restrictions, as the inhabitants thereof respectively; provided that such restrictions shall not extend so far as to prevent the removal of property imported into any State, to any other State, of which the owner is an inhabitant; provided also, that no imposition, duties, or restriction, shall be laid by any State on the property of the United States, or either of them.

If any person guilty of, or charged with, treason, felony, or other high misdemeanor in any State, shall flee from justice, and be found in any of the united States, he shall, upon demand of the governor or executive power of the State from which he fled, be delivered up, and removed to the State having jurisdiction of his offence.

Full faith and credit shall be given, in each of these States, to the records, acts, and judicial proceedings of the courts and magistrates of every other State.

Article V. For the more convenient management of the general interests of the united States, delegates shall be annually appointed in such manner as the legislature of each State shall direct, to meet in Congress on the first Monday in November, in every year, with a power reserved to each State to recall its delegates, or any of them, at any time within the year, and to send others in their stead, for the remainder of the year.

No State shall be represented in Congress by less than two, nor by more than Seven Members; and no person shall be capable of being delegate for more than three years, in any term of Six years; nor shall any person, being a delegate, be capable of holding any office under the united States, for which he, or another for his benefit, receives any salary, fees, or emolument of any kind.

Each State shall maintain its own delegates in a meeting of the States, and while they act as members of the committee of the States.

In determining questions in the united States in Congress assembled, each State shall have one vote.

Freedom of speech and debate in Congress shall not be impeached or questioned in any Court or place out of Congress; and the members of Congress shall be protected in their persons from arrests and imprisonments during the time of their going to and from, and attendance on, Congress, except for treason, felony or breach of the peace.

Article VI. No State, without the consent of the united States, in congress assembled, shall send any embassy to, or receive any embassy from, or enter into any conferrence, agreement, alliance, or treaty, with any King, prince or State; nor shall any person holding any office of profit or trust under the united States, or any of them, accept of any present, emolument, office, or title of any kind whatever, from any king, prince, or foreign State; nor shall the united States, in congress assembled, or any of them, grant any title of nobility.

No two or more States shall enter into any treaty, confederation, or alliance whatever, between them, without the consent of the united States, in Congress assembled, specifying accurately the purposes for which the same is to be entered into, and how long it shall continue.

No State shall lay any imposts or duties, which may interfere with any stipulations in treaties, entered into by the united States, in congress assembled, with any king, prince, or State, in pursuance of any treaties already proposed by congress to the courts of France and Spain.

No vessels of war shall be kept up in time of peace, by any State, except such number only as shall be deemed necessary by the united States, in congress assembled, for the defence of such State, or its trade; nor shall any body of forces be kept up, by any State, in time of peace, except such number only as, in the judgment of the united States, in congress assembled, shall be deemed requisite to garrison the forts necessary for the defence of such State; but every State shall always keep up a well-regulated and disciplined militia, sufficiently armed and accounted, and shall provide and constantly have ready for use, in public stores, a due number of field-pieces and tents, and a proper quantity of arms, ammunition, and camp equipage.

No State shall engage in any war without the consent of the united States, in congress assembled, unless such State be actually invaded by enemies, or shall have received certain advice of a resolution being formed by some nation of Indians to invade such State, and the danger is so imminent as not to admit of a delay till the united States, in congress assembled, can be consulted; nor shall any State grant commissions to any ships or vessels of war, nor letters of marque or reprisal, except it be after a declaration of war by the united States, in congress assembled, and then only against the kingdom or State, and the subjects thereof, against which war has been so declared, and under such regulations as shall be established by the united States, in congress assembled, unless such State be infested by pirates, in which case vessels of war may be fitted out for that occasion, and kept so long as the danger shall continue, or until the united States, in congress assembled, shall determine otherwise.

Article VII. When land forces are raised by any State, for the common defence, all officers of or under the rank of colonel, shall be appointed by the legislature of each State respectively by whom such forces shall be raised, or in such manner as such State shall direct, and all vacancies shall be filled up by the State which first made appointment.

Article VIII. All charges of war, and all other expenses that shall be incurred for the common defence or general welfare, and allowed by the united States, in congress assembled, shall be defrayed out of a common treasury, which shall be supplied by the several States, in proportion to the value of all land within each State, granted to, or surveyed for, any person, as such land and the buildings and improvements thereon shall be estimated, according to such mode as the united States, in congress assembled, shall, from time to time, direct and appoint. The taxes for paying that proportion shall be laid and levied by the authority and direction of the legislatures of the several States, within the time agreed upon by the united States, in congress assembled.

Article IX. The united States, in congress assembled, shall have the sole and exclusive right and power of determining on peace and war, except in the cases mentioned in the sixth Article, of sending and receiving ambassadors; entering into treaties and alliances, provided that no treaty of commerce shall be made, whereby the legislative power of the respective States shall be restrained from imposing such imposts and duties on foreigners, as their own people are subjected to, or from prohibiting the exportation or importation of any species of goods or commodities whatsoever; of establishing rules for deciding, in all cases, what captures on land or water shall be legal, and in what manner prizes taken by land or naval forces in the service of the united Sates, shall be divided or appropriated; of granting letters of marque and reprisal in times of peace; appointing courts for the trial of piracies and felonies committed on the high seas; and establishing courts; for receiving and determining finally appeals in all cases of captures; provided that no member of congress shall be appointed a judge of any of the said courts.

The united States, in congress assembled, shall also be the last resort on appeal, in all disputes and differences now subsisting, or that hereafter may arise between two or more States concerning boundary, jurisdiction, or any other cause whatever; which authority shall always be exercised in the manner following. Whenever the legislative or executive authority, or lawful agent of any State in controversy with another, shall present a petition to congress, stating the matter in question, and praying for a hearing, notice thereof shall be given, by order of congress, to the legislative or executive authority of the other State in controversy, and a day assigned for the appearance of the parties by their lawful agents, who shall then be directed to appoint, by joint consent, commissioners or judges to constitute a court for hearing and determining the matter in question: but if they cannot agree, congress shall name three persons out of each of the united States, and from the list of such persons each party shall alternately strike out one, the petitioners beginning, until the number shall be reduced to thirteen; and from that number not less than seven, nor more than nine names, as congress shall direct, shall, in the presence of congress, be drawn out by lot, and the persons whose names shall be so drawn, or any five of them, shall be commissioners or judges, to hear and finally determine the controversy, so always as a major part of the judges, who shall hear the cause, shall agree in the determination: and if either party shall neglect to attend at the day appointed, without showing reasons which congress shall judge sufficient, or being present, shall refuse to strike, the congress shall proceed to nominate three persons out of each State, and the secretary of congress shall strike in behalf of such party absent or refusing; and the judgment and sentence of the court, to be appointed in the manner before prescribed, shall be final and conclusive; and if any of the parties shall refuse to submit to the authority of such court, or to appear or defend their claim or cause, the court shall nevertheless proceed to pronounce sentence, or judgment, which shall in like manner be final and decisive; the judgment or sentence and other proceedings being in either case transmitted to congress, and lodged among the acts of congress, for the security of the parties concerned: provided that every commissioner, before he sits in judgment, shall take an oath to be administered by one of the judges of the Supreme or Superior court of the State where the cause shall be tried, "well and truly to hear and determine the matter in question, according to the best of his judgment, without favour, affection, or hope of reward: "Provided, also, that no State shall be deprived of territory for the benefit of the united States.

All controversies concerning the private right of soil claimed under different grants of two or more States, whose jurisdictions as they may respect such lands, and the States which passed such grants are adjusted, the said grants or either of them being at the

same time claimed to have originated antecedent to such settlement of jurisdiction, shall, on the petition of either party to the
congress of the united States, be finally determined, as near as
may be, in the same manner as is before prescribed for deciding
disputes respecting territorial jurisdiction between different
States.

The united States, in congress assembled, shall also have the
sole and exclusive right and power of regulating the alloy and
value of coin struck by their own authority, or by that of the
respective States fixing the standard of weights and measures
throughout the united States; regulating the trade and managing
all affairs with the Indians, not members of any of the States;
provided that the legislative right of any State, within its own
limits, be not infringed or violated; establishing and regulating
post-offices from one State to another, throughout all the United
States, and exacting such postage on the papers passing through
the same, as may be requisite to defray the expenses of the said
office; appointing all officers of the land forces in the service of
the united States, excepting regimental officers; appointing all
the officers of the naval forces, and commissioning all officers
whatever in the service of the united States; making rules for the
government and regulation of the said land and naval forces,
and directing their operations.

The united States, in congress assembled, shall have
authority to appoint a committee, to sit in the recess of congress, to be denominated, "A Committee of the States," and
to consist of one delegate from each State; and to appoint such
other committees and civil officers as may be necessary for
managing the general affairs of the united States under their

direction; to appoint one of their number to preside; provided that no person be allowed to serve in the office of president more than one year in any term of three years; to ascertain the necessary sums of money to be raised for the service of the united States, and to appropriate and apply the same for defraying the public expenses; to borrow money or emit bills on the credit of the united States, transmitting every half year to the respective States an account of the sums of money so borrowed or emitted; to build and equip a navy; to agree upon the number of land forces, and to make requisitions from each State for its quota, in proportion to the number of white inhabitants in such State, which requisition shall be binding; and thereupon the Legislature of each State shall appoint the regimental officers, raise the men, and clothe, arm, and equip them, in a soldier-like manner, at the expense of the united States; and the officers and men so clothed, armed, and equipped, shall march to the place appointed, and within the time agreed on by the united States, in congress assembled; but if the united States, in congress assembled, shall, on consideration of circumstances, judge proper that any State should not raise men, or should raise a smaller number than its quota, and that any other State should raise a greater number of men than the quota thereof, such extra number shall be raised, officered, clothed, armed, and equipped in the same manner as the quota of such State, unless the Legislature of such State shall judge that such extra number cannot be safely spared out of the same, in which case they shall raise, officer, clothe, arm, and equip, as many of such extra number as they judge can be safely spared. And the officers and men so clothed, armed, and equipped, shall march to the place appointed, and within the time agreed on by the united States in congress assembled.

The united States, in congress assembled, shall never engage in a war, nor grant letters of marque and reprisal in time of peace, nor enter into any treaties or alliances, nor coin money, nor regulate the value thereof nor ascertain the sums and expenses necessary for the defence and welfare of the united States, or any of them, nor emit bills, nor borrow money on the credit of the united States, nor appropriate money, nor agree upon the number of vessels of war to be built or purchased, or the number of land or sea forces to be raised, nor appoint a commander in chief of the army or navy, unless nine States assent to the same, nor shall a question on any other point, except for adjourning from day to day, be determined, unless by the votes of a majority of the united States in congress assembled.

The congress of the united States shall have power to adjourn to any time within the year, and to any place within the united States, so that no period of adjournment be for a longer duration than the space of six months, and shall publish the journal of their proceedings monthly, except such parts thereof relating to treaties, alliances, or military operations, as in their judgment require secrecy; and the yeas and nays of the delegates of each State, on any question, shall be entered on the journal, when it is desired by any delegate; and the delegates of a State, or any of them, at his or their request, shall be furnished with a transcript of the said journal, except such parts as are above excepted, to lay before the legislatures of the several States.

Article X. The committee of the States, or any nine of them, shall be authorized to execute, in the recess of congress, such of the powers of congress as the united States, in congress assembled, by the consent of nine States, shall, from time to time, think expedient to vest them with; provided that no power be delegated to the said committee, for the exercise of which, by the articles of confederation, the voice of nine States, in the congress of the united States assembled, is requisite.

Article XI. Canada acceding to this confederation, and joining in the measures of the united States, shall be admitted into, and entitled to all the advantages of this union: but no other colony shall be admitted into the same, unless such admission be agreed to by nine States.

Article XII. All bills of credit emitted, monies borrowed, and debts contracted by or under the authority of congress, before the assembling of the united States, in pursuance of the present confederation, shall be deemed and considered as a charge against the united States, for payment and satisfaction whereof the said United States and the public faith are hereby solemnly pledged.

Article XIII. Every State shall abide by the determinations of the united States, in congress assembled, on all questions which by this confederation are submitted to them. And the articles of this confederation shall be inviolably observed by every State, and the Union shall be perpetual; nor shall any alteration at any time hereafter be made in any of them, unless such alteration be agreed to in a congress of the united States, and be afterwards confirmed by the legislatures of every State.

And Whereas it hath pleased the Great Governor of the World to incline the hearts of the legislatures we respectively represent in congress, to approve of, and to authorize us to ratify the said articles of confederation and perpetual union, Know Ye, that we, the undersigned delegates, by virtue of the power and authority to us given for that purpose, do, by these presents, in the name and in behalf of our respective constituents, fully and entirely ratify and confirm each and every of the said articles of confederation and perpetual union, and all and singular the matters and things therein contained. And we do further solemnly plight and engage the faith of our respective constituents, that they shall abide by the determinations of the united States, in congress assembled, on all questions which by the said confederation are submitted to them; and that the articles thereof shall be inviolably observed by the States we respectively represent, and that the Union shall be perpetual. In witness whereof, we have hereunto set our hands, in Congress. Done at Philadelphia, in the State of Pennsylvania, the ninth day of July, in the year of our Lord one thousand seven hundred and seventy eight, and in the third year of the Independence of America.

★ ★ ★

The Declaration of Independence

IN CONGRESS, July 4, 1776.

The unanimous Declaration of the thirteen united States of America,

When in the Course of human events, it becomes necessary for one people to dissolve the political bands which have connected them with another, and to assume among the powers of the earth, the separate and equal station to which the Laws of Nature and of Nature's God entitle them, a decent respect to the opinions of mankind requires that they should declare the causes which impel them to the separation.

We hold these truths to be self-evident, that all men are created equal, that they are endowed by their Creator with certain unalienable Rights, that among these are Life, Liberty and the pursuit of Happiness.—That to secure these rights, Governments are instituted among Men, deriving their just powers from the consent of the governed,—That whenever any Form of Government becomes destructive of these ends, it is the Right of the People to alter or to abolish it, and to institute new Government, laying its foundation on such principles and organizing its powers in such form, as to them shall seem most likely to effect their Safety and Happiness. Prudence, indeed, will dictate that Governments long established should not be changed for light and transient causes; and accordingly all experience hath shewn, that mankind are more disposed to suffer, while evils are sufferable, than to right themselves by abolishing the forms to which they are accustomed. But when a long train of abuses and usurpations, pursuing invariably the same Object evinces a design to reduce them under absolute Despotism, it is their right, it is their duty, to throw off such Government, and to provide new Guards for their future security.—Such has been the patient sufferance of these Colonies; and such is now the necessity which constrains them to alter their former Systems of Government. The history of the present King of Great Britain is a history of repeated injuries and usurpations, all having in direct object the establishment of an absolute Tyranny over these States. To prove this, let Facts be submitted to a candid world.

He has refused his Assent to Laws, the most wholesome and necessary for the public good.

He has forbidden his Governors to pass Laws of immediate and pressing importance, unless suspended in their operation till his Assent should be obtained; and when so suspended, he has utterly neglected to attend to them.

He has refused to pass other Laws for the accommodation of large districts of people, unless those people would relinquish the right of Representation in the Legislature, a right inestimable to them and formidable to tyrants only.

He has called together legislative bodies at places unusual, uncomfortable, and distant from the depository of their public Records, for the sole purpose of fatiguing them into compliance with his measures.

He has dissolved Representative Houses repeatedly, for opposing with manly firmness his invasions on the rights of the people.

He has refused for a long time, after such dissolutions, to cause others to be elected; whereby the Legislative powers, incapable of Annihilation, have returned to the People at large for their exercise; the State remaining in the mean time exposed to all the dangers of invasion from without, and convulsions within.

He has endeavoured to prevent the population of these States; for that purpose obstructing the Laws for Naturalization of Foreigners; refusing to pass others to encourage their migrations hither, and raising the conditions of new Appropriations of Lands.

He has obstructed the Administration of Justice, by refusing his Assent to Laws for establishing Judiciary powers.

He has made Judges dependent on his Will alone, for the tenure of their offices, and the amount and payment of their salaries.

He has erected a multitude of New Offices, and sent hither swarms of Officers to harrass our people, and eat out their substance.

He has kept among us, in times of peace, Standing Armies without the Consent of our legislatures.

He has affected to render the Military independent of and superior to the Civil power.

He has combined with others to subject us to a jurisdiction foreign to our constitution, and unacknowledged by our laws; giving his Assent to their Acts of pretended Legislation:

For Quartering large bodies of armed troops among us:

For protecting them, by a mock Trial, from punishment for any Murders which they should commit on the Inhabitants of these States:

For cutting off our Trade with all parts of the world:

For imposing Taxes on us without our Consent:

For depriving us in many cases, of the benefits of Trial by Jury:

For transporting us beyond Seas to be tried for pretended offences;

For abolishing the free System of English Laws in a neighbouring Province, establishing therein an Arbitrary government, and enlarging its Boundaries so as to render it at once an example and fit instrument for introducing the same absolute rule into these Colonies:

For taking away our Charters, abolishing our most valuable Laws, and altering fundamentally the Forms of our Governments:

For suspending our own Legislatures, and declaring themselves invested with power to legislate for us in all cases whatsoever.

He has abdicated Government here, by declaring us out of his Protection and waging War against us.

He has plundered our seas, ravaged our Coasts, burnt our towns, and destroyed the lives of our people.

He is at this time transporting large Armies of foreign Mercenaries to compleat the works of death, desolation and tyranny, already begun with circumstances of Cruelty & perfidy scarcely paralleled in the most barbarous ages, and totally unworthy the Head of a civilized nation.

He has constrained our fellow Citizens taken Captive on the high Seas to bear Arms against their Country, to become the executioners of their friends and Brethren, or to fall themselves by their Hands.

He has excited domestic insurrections amongst us, and has endeavoured to bring on the inhabitants of our frontiers, the merciless Indian Savages, whose known rule of warfare, is an undistinguished destruction of all ages, sexes and conditions.

In every stage of these Oppressions We have Petitioned for Redress in the most humble terms: Our repeated Petitions have been answered only by repeated injury. A Prince whose character is thus marked by every act which may define a Tyrant, is unfit to be the ruler of a free people.

Nor have We been wanting in attentions to our Brittish brethren. We have warned them from time to time of attempts by their legislature to extend an unwarrantable jurisdiction over us. We have reminded them of the circumstances of our emigration and settlement here. We have appealed to their native justice and magnanimity, and we have conjured them by the ties of our common kindred to disavow these usurpations, which, would inevitably interrupt our connections and correspondence. They too have been deaf to the voice of justice and of consanguinity. We must, therefore, acquiesce in the necessity, which denounces our Separation, and hold them, as we hold the rest of mankind, Enemies in War, in Peace Friends.

We, therefore, the Representatives of the united States of America, in General Congress, Assembled, appealing to the Supreme Judge of the world for the rectitude of our intentions, do, in the Name, and by Authority of the good People of these Colonies, solemnly publish and declare, That these United Colonies are, and of Right ought to be Free and Independent States; that they are Absolved from all Allegiance to the British Crown, and that all political connection between them and the State of Great Britain, is and ought to be totally dissolved; and that as Free and Independent States, they have full Power to levy War, conclude Peace, contract Alliances, establish Commerce, and to do all other Acts and Things which Independent States may of right do. And for the support of this Declaration, with a firm reliance on the protection of divine Providence, we mutually pledge to each other our Lives, our Fortunes and our sacred Honor.

The 56 signatures on the Declaration appear in the positions indicated:

Column I

Georgia
Button Gwinnett

Lyman Hall
George Walton

Column 2

North Carolina
William Hooper
Joseph Hewes
John Penn
South Carolina
Edward Rutledge
Thomas Heyward, Jr.
Thomas Lynch, Jr.
Arthur Middleton

Column 3

Massachusetts
John Hancock
Maryland
Samuel Chase
William Paca
Thomas Stone
Charles Carroll of Carrollton
Virginia
George Wythe
Richard Henry Lee
Thomas Jefferson
Benjamin Harrison

Thomas Nelson, Jr.
Francis Lightfoot Lee
Carter Braxton

Column 4

Pennsylvania
Robert Morris
Benjamin Rush
Benjamin Franklin
John Morton
George Clymer
James Smith
George Taylor
James Wilson
George Ross
Delaware
Caesar Rodney
George Read
Thomas McKean

Column 5

New York
William Floyd
Philip Livingston
Francis Lewis
Lewis Morris
New Jersey

Richard Stockton
John Witherspoon
Francis Hopkinson
John Hart
Abraham Clark

Column 6

New Hampshire
Josiah Bartlett
William Whipple
Matthew Thornton
Massachusetts
Samuel Adams
John Adams
Robert Treat Paine
Elbridge Gerry
Rhode Island
Stephen Hopkins
William Ellery
Connecticut
Roger Sherman
Samuel Huntington
William Williams
Oliver Wolcott

★ ★ ★

The Constitution of the United States

We the People of the United States, in Order to form a more perfect Union, establish Justice, insure domestic Tranquility, provide for the common defence, promote the general Welfare, and secure the Blessings of Liberty to ourselves and our Posterity, do ordain and establish this Constitution for the United States of America.

Article I

Section 1

All legislative Powers herein granted shall be vested in a Congress of the United States, which shall consist of a Senate and House of Representatives.

Section 2

The House of Representatives shall be composed of Members chosen every second Year by the People of the several States, and the Electors in each State shall have the Qualifications requisite for Electors of the most numerous Branch of the State Legislature.

No Person shall be a Representative who shall not have attained to the Age of twenty five Years, and been seven Years a Citizen of the United States, and who shall not, when elected, be an Inhabitant of that State in which he shall be chosen.

Representatives and direct Taxes shall be apportioned among the several States which may be included within this Union, according to their respective Numbers, which shall be determined by adding to the whole Number of free Persons, including those bound to Service for a Term of Years, and excluding Indians not taxed, three fifths of all other Persons. The actual Enumeration shall be made within three Years after the first Meeting of the Congress of the United States, and within every subsequent Term of ten Years, in such Manner as they shall by Law direct. The Number of Representatives shall not exceed one for every thirty Thousand, but each State shall have at Least one Representative; and until such enumeration shall be made, the State of New Hampshire shall be entitled to chuse three, Massachusetts eight,

Rhode-Island and Providence Plantations one, Connecticut five, New-York six, New Jersey four, Pennsylvania eight, Delaware one, Maryland six, Virginia ten, North Carolina five, South Carolina five, and Georgia three.

When vacancies happen in the Representation from any State, the Executive Authority thereof shall issue Writs of Election to fill such Vacancies.

The House of Representatives shall chuse their Speaker and other Officers; and shall have the sole Power of Impeachment.

Section 3

The Senate of the United States shall be composed of two Senators from each State, chosen by the Legislature thereof for six Years; and each Senator shall have one Vote.

Immediately after they shall be assembled in Consequence of the first Election, they shall be divided as equally as may be into three Classes. The Seats of the Senators of the first Class shall be vacated at the Expiration of the second Year, of the second Class at the Expiration of the fourth Year, and of the third Class at the Expiration of the sixth Year, so that one third may be chosen every second Year; and if Vacancies happen by Resignation, or otherwise, during the Recess of the Legislature of any State, the Executive thereof may make temporary Appointments until the next Meeting of the Legislature, which shall then fill such Vacancies.

No Person shall be a Senator who shall not have attained to the Age of thirty Years, and been nine Years a Citizen of the United States, and who shall not, when elected, be an Inhabitant of that State for which he shall be chosen.

The Vice President of the United States shall be President of the Senate, but shall have no Vote, unless they be equally divided.

The Senate shall chuse their other Officers, and also a President pro tempore, in the Absence of the Vice President, or when he shall exercise the Office of President of the United States.

The Senate shall have the sole Power to try all Impeachments. When sitting for that Purpose, they shall be on Oath or Affirmation. When the President of the United States is tried, the Chief Justice shall preside: And no Person shall be convicted without the Concurrence of two thirds of the Members present.

Judgment in Cases of Impeachment shall not extend further than to removal from Office, and disqualification to hold and enjoy any Office of honor, Trust or Profit under the United States: but the Party convicted shall nevertheless be liable and subject to Indictment, Trial, Judgment and Punishment, according to Law.

Section 4

The Times, Places and Manner of holding Elections for Senators and Representatives, shall be prescribed in each State by the Legislature thereof; but the Congress may at any time by Law make or alter such Regulations, except as to the Places of chusing Senators.

The Congress shall assemble at least once in every Year, and such Meeting shall be on the first Monday in December, unless they shall by Law appoint a different Day.

Section 5

Each House shall be the Judge of the Elections, Returns and Qualifications of its own Members, and a Majority of each shall constitute a Quorum to do Business; but a smaller Number may adjourn from day to day, and may be authorized to compel the Attendance of absent Members, in such Manner, and under such Penalties as each House may provide.

Each House may determine the Rules of its Proceedings, punish its Members for disorderly Behaviour, and, with the Concurrence of two thirds, expel a Member.

Each House shall keep a Journal of its Proceedings, and from time to time publish the same, excepting such Parts as may in their Judgment require Secrecy; and the Yeas and Nays of the Members of either House on any question shall, at the Desire of one fifth of those Present, be entered on the Journal.

Neither House, during the Session of Congress, shall, without the Consent of the other, adjourn for more than three days, nor to any other Place than that in which the two Houses shall be sitting.

Section 6

The Senators and Representatives shall receive a Compensation for their Services, to be ascertained by Law, and paid out of the Treasury of the United States. They shall in all Cases, except Treason, Felony and Breach of the Peace, be privileged from Arrest during their Attendance at the Session of their respective Houses, and in going to and returning from the same; and for any Speech or Debate in either House, they shall not be questioned in any other Place.

No Senator or Representative shall, during the Time for which he was elected, be appointed to any civil Office under the Authority of the United States, which shall have been created, or the Emoluments whereof shall have been encreased during such time; and no Person holding any Office under the United States, shall be a Member of either House during his Continuance in Office.

Section 7

All Bills for raising Revenue shall originate in the House of Representatives; but the Senate may propose or concur with Amendments as on other Bills.

Every Bill which shall have passed the House of Representatives and the Senate, shall, before it become a Law, be presented to the President of the United States: If he approve he shall sign it, but if not he shall return it, with his Objections to that House in which it shall have originated, who shall enter the Objections at large on their Journal, and proceed to reconsider it. If after such Reconsideration two thirds of that House shall agree to pass the Bill, it shall be sent, together with the Objections, to the other House, by which it shall likewise be reconsidered, and if approved by two thirds of that House, it shall become a Law. But in all such Cases the Votes of both Houses shall be determined by yeas and Nays, and the Names of the Persons voting for and against the Bill shall be entered on the Journal of each House respectively. If any Bill shall not be returned by the President within ten Days (Sundays excepted) after it shall have been presented to him, the Same shall be a Law, in like Manner as if he had signed it, unless the Congress by their Adjournment prevent its Return, in which Case it shall not be a Law.

Every Order, Resolution, or Vote to which the Concurrence of the Senate and House of Representatives may be necessary (except on a question of Adjournment) shall be presented to the President of the United States; and before the Same shall take Effect, shall be approved by him, or being disapproved by him, shall be repassed by two thirds of the Senate and House of Representatives, according to the Rules and Limitations prescribed in the Case of a Bill.

Section 8

The Congress shall have Power To lay and collect Taxes, Duties, Imposts and Excises, to pay the Debts and provide for the common Defence and general Welfare of the United States; but all Duties, Imposts and Excises shall be uniform throughout the United States;

To borrow Money on the credit of the United States;

To regulate Commerce with foreign Nations, and among the several States, and with the Indian Tribes;

To establish an uniform Rule of Naturalization, and uniform Laws on the subject of Bankruptcies throughout the United States;

To coin Money, regulate the Value thereof, and of foreign Coin, and fix the Standard of Weights and Measures;

To provide for the Punishment of counterfeiting the Securities and current Coin of the United States;

To establish Post Offices and Post Roads;

To promote the Progress of Science and useful Arts, by securing for limited Times to Authors and Inventors the exclusive Right to their respective Writings and Discoveries;

To constitute Tribunals inferior to the supreme Court;

To define and punish Piracies and Felonies committed on the high Seas, and Offences against the Law of Nations;

To declare War, grant Letters of Marque and Reprisal, and make Rules concerning Captures on Land and Water;

To raise and support Armies, but no Appropriation of Money to that Use shall be for a longer Term than two Years;

To provide and maintain a Navy;

To make Rules for the Government and Regulation of the land and naval Forces;

To provide for calling forth the Militia to execute the Laws of the Union, suppress Insurrections and repel Invasions;

To provide for organizing, arming, and disciplining, the Militia, and for governing such Part of them as may be employed in the Service of the United States, reserving to the States respectively, the Appointment of the Officers, and the Authority of training the Militia according to the discipline prescribed by Congress;

To exercise exclusive Legislation in all Cases whatsoever, over such District (not exceeding ten Miles square) as may, by Cession of particular States, and the Acceptance of Congress, become the Seat of the Government of the United States, and to exercise like Authority over all Places purchased by the Consent of the Legislature of the State in which the Same shall be, for the Erection of Forts, Magazines, Arsenals, dock-Yards, and other needful Buildings;—And

To make all Laws which shall be necessary and proper for carrying into Execution the foregoing Powers, and all other Powers vested by this Constitution in the Government of the United States, or in any Department or Officer thereof.

Section 9

The Migration or Importation of such Persons as any of the States now existing shall think proper to admit, shall not be prohibited by the Congress prior to the Year one thousand eight hundred and eight, but a Tax or duty may be imposed on such Importation, not exceeding ten dollars for each Person.

The Privilege of the Writ of Habeas Corpus shall not be suspended, unless when in Cases of Rebellion or Invasion the public Safety may require it.

No Bill of Attainder or ex post facto Law shall be passed.

No Capitation, or other direct, Tax shall be laid, unless in Proportion to the Census or enumeration herein before directed to be taken.

No Tax or Duty shall be laid on Articles exported from any State.

No Preference shall be given by any Regulation of Commerce or Revenue to the Ports of one State over those of another; nor shall Vessels bound to, or from, one State, be obliged to enter, clear, or pay Duties in another.

No Money shall be drawn from the Treasury, but in Consequence of Appropriations made by Law; and a regular Statement and Account of the Receipts and Expenditures of all public Money shall be published from time to time.

No Title of Nobility shall be granted by the United States: And no Person holding any Office of Profit or Trust under them, shall, without the Consent of the Congress, accept of any present, Emolument, Office, or Title, of any kind whatever, from any King, Prince, or foreign State.

Section 10

No State shall enter into any Treaty, Alliance, or Confederation; grant Letters of Marque and Reprisal; coin Money; emit Bills of Credit; make any Thing but gold and silver

Coin a Tender in Payment of Debts; pass any Bill of Attainder, ex post facto Law, or Law impairing the Obligation of Contracts, or grant any Title of Nobility.

No State shall, without the Consent of the Congress, lay any Imposts or Duties on Imports or Exports, except what may be absolutely necessary for executing it's inspection Laws: and the net Produce of all Duties and Imposts, laid by any State on Imports or Exports, shall be for the Use of the Treasury of the United States; and all such Laws shall be subject to the Revision and Controul of the Congress.

No State shall, without the Consent of Congress, lay any Duty of Tonnage, keep Troops, or Ships of War in time of Peace, enter into any Agreement or Compact with another State, or with a foreign Power, or engage in War, unless actually invaded, or in such imminent Danger as will not admit of delay.

Article II

Section I

The executive Power shall be vested in a President of the United States of America. He shall hold his Office during the Term of four Years, and, together with the Vice President, chosen for the same Term, be elected, as follows:

Each State shall appoint, in such Manner as the Legislature thereof may direct, a Number of Electors, equal to the whole Number of Senators and Representatives to which the State may be entitled in the Congress: but no Senator or Representative, or

Person holding an Office of Trust or Profit under the United States, shall be appointed an Elector.

The Electors shall meet in their respective States, and vote by Ballot for two Persons, of whom one at least shall not be an Inhabitant of the same State with themselves. And they shall make a List of all the Persons voted for, and of the Number of Votes for each; which List they shall sign and certify, and transmit sealed to the Seat of the Government of the United States, directed to the President of the Senate. The President of the Senate shall, in the Presence of the Senate and House of Representatives, open all the Certificates, and the Votes shall then be counted. The Person having the greatest Number of Votes shall be the President, if such Number be a Majority of the whole Number of Electors appointed; and if there be more than one who have such Majority, and have an equal Number of Votes, then the House of Representatives shall immediately chuse by Ballot one of them for President; and if no Person have a Majority, then from the five highest on the List the said House shall in like Manner chuse the President. But in chusing the President, the Votes shall be taken by States, the Representation from each State having one Vote; A quorum for this purpose shall consist of a Member or Members from two thirds of the States, and a Majority of all the States shall be necessary to a Choice. In every Case, after the Choice of the President, the Person having the greatest Number of Votes of the Electors shall be the Vice President. But if there should remain two or more who have equal Votes, the Senate shall chuse from them by Ballot the Vice President.

The Congress may determine the Time of chusing the Electors, and the Day on which they shall give their Votes; which Day shall be the same throughout the United States.

No Person except a natural born Citizen, or a Citizen of the United States, at the time of the Adoption of this Constitution, shall be eligible to the Office of President; neither shall any Person be eligible to that Office who shall not have attained to the Age of thirty five Years, and been fourteen Years a Resident within the United States.

In Case of the Removal of the President from Office, or of his Death, Resignation, or Inability to discharge the Powers and Duties of the said Office, the Same shall devolve on the Vice President, and the Congress may by Law provide for the Case of Removal, Death, Resignation or Inability, both of the President and Vice President, declaring what Officer shall then act as President, and such Officer shall act accordingly, until the Disability be removed, or a President shall be elected.

The President shall, at stated Times, receive for his Services, a Compensation, which shall neither be increased nor diminished during the Period for which he shall have been elected, and he shall not receive within that Period any other Emolument from the United States, or any of them.

Before he enter on the Execution of his Office, he shall take the following Oath or Affirmation:—"I do solemnly swear (or affirm) that I will faithfully execute the Office of President of the United States, and will to the best of my Ability, preserve, protect and defend the Constitution of the United States."

Section 2

The President shall be Commander in Chief of the Army and Navy of the United States, and of the Militia of the several States, when called into the actual Service of the United States; he may require the Opinion, in writing, of the principal Officer in each of the executive Departments, upon any Subject relating to the Duties of their respective Offices, and he shall have Power to grant Reprieves and Pardons for Offences against the United States, except in Cases of Impeachment.

He shall have Power, by and with the Advice and Consent of the Senate, to make Treaties, provided two thirds of the Senators present concur; and he shall nominate, and by and with the Advice and Consent of the Senate, shall appoint Ambassadors, other public Ministers and Consuls, Judges of the supreme Court, and all other Officers of the United States, whose Appointments are not herein otherwise provided for, and which shall be established by Law: but the Congress may by Law vest the Appointment of such inferior Officers, as they think proper, in the President alone, in the Courts of Law, or in the Heads of Departments.

The President shall have Power to fill up all Vacancies that may happen during the Recess of the Senate, by granting Commissions which shall expire at the End of their next Session.

Section 3

He shall from time to time give to the Congress Information of the State of the Union, and recommend to their Consideration such Measures as he shall judge necessary and expedient; he may, on extraordinary Occasions, convene both Houses, or either of them, and in Case of Disagreement between them, with Respect to the Time of Adjournment, he may adjourn them to such Time as he shall think proper; he shall receive Ambassadors and other public Ministers; he shall take Care that the Laws be faithfully executed, and shall Commission all the Officers of the United States.

Section 4

The President, Vice President and all civil Officers of the United States, shall be removed from Office on Impeachment for, and Conviction of, Treason, Bribery, or other high Crimes and Misdemeanors.

Article III

Section 1

The judicial Power of the United States shall be vested in one supreme Court, and in such inferior Courts as the Congress may from time to time ordain and establish. The Judges, both of the supreme and inferior Courts, shall hold their Offices during good Behaviour, and shall, at stated Times, receive for their Services a Compensation, which shall not be diminished during their Continuance in Office.

Section 2

The judicial Power shall extend to all Cases, in Law and Equity, arising under this Constitution, the Laws of the United States, and Treaties made, or which shall be made, under their Authority;—to all Cases affecting Ambassadors, other public

Ministers and Consuls;—to all Cases of admiralty and maritime Jurisdiction;—to Controversies to which the United States shall be a Party;—to Controversies between two or more States;—between a State and Citizens of another State;—between Citizens of different States;—between Citizens of the same State claiming Lands under Grants of different States, and between a State, or the Citizens thereof, and foreign States, Citizens or Subjects.

In all Cases affecting Ambassadors, other public Ministers and Consuls, and those in which a State shall be Party, the supreme Court shall have original Jurisdiction. In all the other Cases before mentioned, the supreme Court shall have appellate Jurisdiction, both as to Law and Fact, with such Exceptions, and under such Regulations as the Congress shall make.

The Trial of all Crimes, except in Cases of Impeachment, shall be by Jury; and such Trial shall be held in the State where the said Crimes shall have been committed; but when not committed within any State, the Trial shall be at such Place or Places as the Congress may by Law have directed.

Section 3

Treason against the United States, shall consist only in levying War against them, or in adhering to their Enemies, giving them Aid and Comfort. No Person shall be convicted of Treason unless on the Testimony of two Witnesses to the same overt Act, or on Confession in open Court.

The Congress shall have Power to declare the Punishment of Treason, but no Attainder of Treason shall work Corruption of Blood, or Forfeiture except during the Life of the Person attainted.

Article IV

Section 1

Full Faith and Credit shall be given in each State to the public Acts, Records, and judicial Proceedings of every other State. And the Congress may by general Laws prescribe the Manner in which such Acts, Records and Proceedings shall be proved, and the Effect thereof.

Section 2

The Citizens of each State shall be entitled to all Privileges and Immunities of Citizens in the several States.

A Person charged in any State with Treason, Felony, or other Crime, who shall flee from Justice, and be found in another State, shall on Demand of the executive Authority of the State from which he fled, be delivered up, to be removed to the State having Jurisdiction of the Crime.

No Person held to Service or Labour in one State, under the Laws thereof, escaping into another, shall, in Consequence of any Law or Regulation therein, be discharged from such Service or Labour, but shall be delivered up on Claim of the Party to whom such Service or Labour may be due.

Section 3

New States may be admitted by the Congress into this Union; but no new State shall be formed or erected within the Jurisdiction of any other State; nor any State be formed by the Junction of two or more States, or Parts of States, without the Consent of the Legislatures of the States concerned as well as of the Congress.

The Congress shall have Power to dispose of and make all needful Rules and Regulations respecting the Territory or other Property belonging to the United States; and nothing in this Constitution shall be so construed as to Prejudice any Claims of the United States, or of any particular State.

Section 4

The United States shall guarantee to every State in this Union a Republican Form of Government, and shall protect each of them against Invasion; and on Application of the Legislature, or of the Executive (when the Legislature cannot be convened), against domestic Violence.

Article V

The Congress, whenever two thirds of both Houses shall deem it necessary, shall propose Amendments to this Constitution, or, on the Application of the Legislatures of two thirds of the several States, shall call a Convention for proposing Amendments, which, in either Case, shall be valid to all Intents and Purposes, as Part of this Constitution, when ratified by the Legislatures of three fourths of the several States, or by Conventions in three fourths thereof, as the one or the other Mode of Ratification may be proposed by the Congress; Provided that no Amendment which may be made prior to the Year One thousand eight hundred and eight shall in any Manner affect the first and fourth Clauses in the Ninth Section of the first Article; and that no State, without its Consent, shall be deprived of its equal Suffrage in the Senate.

Article VI

All Debts contracted and Engagements entered into, before the Adoption of this Constitution, shall be as valid against the United States under this Constitution, as under the Confederation.

This Constitution, and the Laws of the United States which shall be made in Pursuance thereof; and all Treaties made, or which shall be made, under the Authority of the United States, shall be the supreme Law of the Land; and the Judges in every State shall be bound thereby, any Thing in the Constitution or Laws of any State to the Contrary notwithstanding.

The Senators and Representatives before mentioned, and the Members of the several State Legislatures, and all executive and judicial Officers, both of the United States and of the several States, shall be bound by Oath or Affirmation, to support this Constitution; but no religious Test shall ever be required as a Qualification to any Office or public Trust under the United States.

Article VII

The Ratification of the Conventions of nine States, shall be sufficient for the Establishment of this Constitution between the States so ratifying the Same.

The Word, "the," being interlined between the seventh and eighth Lines of the first Page, the Word "Thirty" being partly written on an Erazure in the fifteenth Line of the first Page, The Words "is tried" being interlined between the thirty second and thirty third Lines of the first Page and the Word "the" being interlined between the forty third and forty fourth Lines of the second Page.

Attest William Jackson Secretary

Done in Convention by the Unanimous Consent of the States present the Seventeenth Day of September in the Year of our Lord one thousand seven hundred and Eighty seven and of the Independence of the United States of America the Twelfth In witness whereof We have hereunto subscribed our Names,

G°. Washington
Presidt and deputy from Virginia

Delaware
Geo: Read
Gunning Bedford jun
John Dickinson
Richard Bassett
Jaco: Broom

Maryland
James McHenry
Dan of St Thos. Jenifer
Danl. Carroll

Virginia
John Blair
James Madison Jr.

North Carolina
Wm. Blount

Richd. Dobbs Spaight
Hu Williamson

South Carolina
J. Rutledge
Charles Cotesworth Pinckney
Charles Pinckney
Pierce Butler

Georgia
William Few
Abr Baldwin

New Hampshire
John Langdon
Nicholas Gilman

Massachusetts
Nathaniel Gorham
Rufus King

Connecticut
Wm. Saml. Johnson
Roger Sherman

New York
Alexander Hamilton

New Jersey
Wil: Livingston

David Brearley
Wm. Paterson
Jona: Dayton

Pennsylvania

B Franklin
Thomas Mifflin
Robt. Morris
Geo. Clymer
Thos. FitzSimons
Jared Ingersoll
James Wilson
Gouv Morris

Amendment I

Congress shall make no law respecting an establishment of religion, or prohibiting the free exercise thereof; or abridging the freedom of speech, or of the press; or the right of the people peaceably to assemble, and to petition the Government for a redress of grievances.

Amendment II

A well regulated Militia, being necessary to the security of a free State, the right of the people to keep and bear Arms, shall not be infringed.

Amendment III

No Soldier shall, in time of peace be quartered in any house, without the consent of the Owner, nor in time of war, but in a manner to be prescribed by law.

Amendment IV

The right of the people to be secure in their persons, houses, papers, and effects, against unreasonable searches and seizures, shall not be violated, and no Warrants shall issue, but upon probable cause, supported by Oath or affirmation, and particularly describing the place to be searched, and the persons or things to be seized.

Amendment V

No person shall be held to answer for a capital, or otherwise infamous crime, unless on a presentment or indictment of a Grand Jury, except in cases arising in the land or naval forces, or in the Militia, when in actual service in time of War or public danger; nor shall any person be subject for the same offence to be twice put in jeopardy of life or limb; nor shall be compelled in any criminal case to be a witness against himself, nor be deprived of life, liberty, or property, without due process of law; nor shall private property be taken for public use, without just compensation.

Amendment VI

In all criminal prosecutions, the accused shall enjoy the right to a speedy and public trial, by an impartial jury of the State and district wherein the crime shall have been committed, which district shall have been previously ascertained by law, and to be informed of the nature and cause of the accusation; to be confronted with the witnesses against him; to have compulsory process for obtaining witnesses in his favor, and to have the Assistance of Counsel for his defence.

Amendment VII

In Suits at common law, where the value in controversy shall exceed twenty dollars, the right of trial by jury shall be preserved, and no fact tried by a jury, shall be otherwise re-examined in any Court of the United States, than according to the rules of the common law.

Amendment VIII

Excessive bail shall not be required, nor excessive fines imposed, nor cruel and unusual punishments inflicted.

Amendment IX

The enumeration in the Constitution, of certain rights, shall not be construed to deny or disparage others retained by the people.

Amendment X

The powers not delegated to the United States by the Constitution, nor prohibited by it to the States, are reserved to the States respectively, or to the people.

Amendment XI

Passed by Congress March 4, 1794. Ratified February 7, 1795.

The Judicial power of the United States shall not be construed to extend to any suit in law or equity, commenced or prosecuted against one of the United States by Citizens of another State, or by Citizens or Subjects of any Foreign State.

Amendment XII

Passed by Congress December 9, 1803. Ratified June 15, 1804.

The Electors shall meet in their respective states and vote by ballot for President and Vice-President, one of whom, at least, shall not be an inhabitant of the same state with themselves; they shall name in their ballots the person voted for as President, and in distinct ballots the person voted for as Vice-President, and they shall make distinct lists of all persons voted for as President, and of all persons voted for as Vice-President, and of the number of votes for each, which lists they shall sign and certify, and transmit sealed to the seat of the government of the United States, directed to the President of the Senate;—the President of the Senate shall, in the presence of the Senate and House of Representatives, open all the certificates and the votes shall then be counted;—The person having the greatest number of votes for President, shall be the President, if such number be a majority of the whole number of Electors appointed; and if no person have such majority, then from the persons having the highest numbers not exceeding three on the list of those voted for as President, the House of Representatives shall choose immediately, by ballot, the President. But in choosing the President, the votes shall be taken by states, the representation from each state having one vote; a quorum for this purpose shall consist of a member or members from two-thirds of the states, and a majority of all the states shall be necessary to a choice. [And if the House of Representatives shall not choose a President whenever the right of choice shall devolve upon them, before the fourth day of March next following, then the Vice-President shall act as President, as in case of the death or other constitutional disability of the President.] The person having the greatest number of votes as Vice-President, shall be the Vice-President, if such number be a majority of the whole number of Electors appointed, and if no person have a majority, then from the two highest numbers on the list, the Senate shall choose the Vice-President; a quorum for the purpose shall consist of two-thirds of the whole number of Senators, and a majority of the whole number shall be necessary to a choice. But no person constitutionally ineligible to the office of President shall be eligible to that of Vice-President of the United States.

Amendment XIII

Passed by Congress January 31, 1865. Ratified December 6, 1865.

Section 1

Neither slavery nor involuntary servitude, except as a punishment for crime whereof the party shall have been duly convicted, shall exist within the United States, or any place subject to their jurisdiction.

Section 2

Congress shall have power to enforce this article by appropriate legislation.

Amendment XIV

Passed by Congress June 13, 1866. Ratified July 9, 1868.

Section 1

All persons born or naturalized in the United States, and subject to the jurisdiction thereof, are citizens of the United States and of the State wherein they reside. No State shall make or enforce any law which shall abridge the privileges or immunities of citizens of the United States; nor shall any State deprive any person of life, liberty, or property, without due process of law; nor deny to any person within its jurisdiction the equal protection of the laws.

Section 2

Representatives shall be apportioned among the several States according to their respective numbers, counting the whole number of persons in each State, excluding Indians not taxed. But when the right to vote at any election for the choice of electors for President and Vice-President of the United States, Representatives in Congress, the Executive and Judicial officers of a State, or the members of the Legislature thereof, is denied to any of the male inhabitants of such State, being twenty-one years of age, and citizens of the United States, or in any way abridged, except for participation in rebellion, or other crime, the basis of representation therein shall be reduced in the proportion which the number of such male citizens shall bear to the whole number of male citizens twenty-one years of age in such State.

Section 3

No person shall be a Senator or Representative in Congress, or elector of President and Vice-President, or hold any office, civil or military, under the United States, or under any State, who, having previously taken an oath, as a member of Congress, or as an officer of the United States, or as a member of any State legislature, or as an executive or judicial officer of any State, to support the Constitution of the United States, shall have engaged in insurrection or rebellion against the same, or given aid or comfort to the enemies thereof. But Congress may by a vote of two-thirds of each House, remove such disability.

Section 4

The validity of the public debt of the United States, authorized by law, including debts incurred for payment of pensions and bounties for services in suppressing insurrection or rebellion, shall not be questioned. But neither the United States nor any State shall assume or pay any debt or obligation incurred in aid of insurrection or rebellion against the United States, or any claim for the loss or emancipation of any slave; but all such debts, obligations and claims shall be held illegal and void.

Section 5

The Congress shall have the power to enforce, by appropriate legislation, the provisions of this article.

Amendment XV

Passed by Congress February 26, 1869. Ratified February 3, 1870.

Section 1

The right of citizens of the United States to vote shall not be denied or abridged by the United States or by any State on account of race, color, or previous condition of servitude.

Section 2

The Congress shall have the power to enforce this article by appropriate legislation.

Amendment XVI

Passed by Congress July 2, 1909. Ratified February 3, 1913.

The Congress shall have power to lay and collect taxes on incomes, from whatever source derived, without apportionment among the several States, and without regard to any census or enumeration.

Amendment XVII

Passed by Congress May 13, 1912. Ratified April 8, 1913.

The Senate of the United States shall be composed of two Senators from each State, elected by the people thereof, for six years; and each Senator shall have one vote. The electors in each State shall have the qualifications requisite for electors of the most numerous branch of the State legislatures.

When vacancies happen in the representation of any State in the Senate, the executive authority of such State shall issue writs of election to fill such vacancies: Provided, That the legislature of any State may empower the executive thereof to make temporary appointments until the people fill the vacancies by election as the legislature may direct.

This amendment shall not be so construed as to affect the election or term of any Senator chosen before it becomes valid as part of the Constitution.

Amendment XVIII

Passed by Congress December 18, 1917. Ratified January 16, 1919. Repealed by amendment 21.

Section 1

After one year from the ratification of this article the manufacture, sale, or transportation of intoxicating liquors within, the importation thereof into, or the exportation thereof from the United States and all territory subject to the jurisdiction thereof for beverage purposes is hereby prohibited.

Section 2

The Congress and the several States shall have concurrent power to enforce this article by appropriate legislation.

Section 3

This article shall be inoperative unless it shall have been ratified as an amendment to the Constitution by the legislatures of the several States, as provided in the Constitution, within seven years from the date of the submission hereof to the States by the Congress.

Amendment XIX

Passed by Congress June 4, 1919. Ratified August 18, 1920.

The right of citizens of the United States to vote shall not be denied or abridged by the United States or by any State on account of sex.

Congress shall have power to enforce this article by appropriate legislation.

Amendment XX

Passed by Congress March 2, 1932. Ratified January 23, 1933.

Section 1

The terms of the President and the Vice President shall end at noon on the 20th day of January, and the terms of Senators and Representatives at noon on the 3d day of January, of the years in which such terms would have ended if this article had not been ratified; and the terms of their successors shall then begin.

Section 2

The Congress shall assemble at least once in every year, and such meeting shall begin at noon on the 3d day of January, unless they shall by law appoint a different day.

Section 3

If, at the time fixed for the beginning of the term of the President, the President elect shall have died, the Vice President elect shall become President. If a President shall not have been chosen before the time fixed for the beginning of his term, or if the President elect shall have failed to qualify, then the Vice President elect shall act as President until a President shall have qualified; and the Congress may by law provide for the case wherein neither a President elect nor a Vice President shall have qualified, declaring who shall then act as President, or the manner in which one who is to act shall be selected, and such person shall act accordingly until a President or Vice President shall have qualified.

Section 4

The Congress may by law provide for the case of the death of any of the persons from whom the House of Representatives may choose a President whenever the right of choice shall have devolved upon them, and for the case of the death of any of the persons from whom the Senate may choose a Vice President whenever the right of choice shall have devolved upon them.

Section 5

Sections 1 and 2 shall take effect on the 15th day of October following the ratification of this article.

Section 6

This article shall be inoperative unless it shall have been ratified as an amendment to the Constitution by the legislatures of three-fourths of the several States within seven years from the date of its submission.

Amendment XXI

Passed by Congress February 20, 1933. Ratified December 5, 1933.

Section 1

The eighteenth article of amendment to the Constitution of the United States is hereby repealed.

Section 2

The transportation or importation into any State, Territory, or Possession of the United States for delivery or use therein of intoxicating liquors, in violation of the laws thereof, is hereby prohibited.

Section 3

This article shall be inoperative unless it shall have been ratified as an amendment to the Constitution by conventions in the several States, as provided in the Constitution, within seven years from the date of the submission hereof to the States by the Congress.

Amendment XXII

Passed by Congress March 21, 1947. Ratified February 27, 1951.

Section 1

No person shall be elected to the office of the President more than twice, and no person who has held the office of President, or acted as President, for more than two years of a term to which some other person was elected President shall be elected to the office of President more than once. But this Article shall not apply to any person holding the office of President when this Article was proposed by Congress, and shall not prevent any person who may be holding the office of President, or acting as President, during the term within which this Article becomes operative from holding the office of President or acting as President during the remainder of such term.

Section 2

This article shall be inoperative unless it shall have been ratified as an amendment to the Constitution by the legislatures of three-fourths of the several States within seven years from the date of its submission to the States by the Congress.

Amendment XXIII

Passed by Congress June 16, 1960. Ratified March 29, 1961.

Section 1

The District constituting the seat of Government of the United States shall appoint in such manner as Congress may direct:

A number of electors of President and Vice President equal to the whole number of Senators and Representatives in Congress to which the District would be entitled if it were a State, but in no event more than the least populous State; they shall be in addition to those appointed by the States, but they shall be considered, for the purposes of the election of President and Vice President, to be electors appointed by a State; and they shall meet in the District and perform such duties as provided by the twelfth article of amendment.

Section 2

The Congress shall have power to enforce this article by appropriate legislation.

Amendment XXIV

Passed by Congress August 27, 1962. Ratified January 23, 1964.

Section 1

The right of citizens of the United States to vote in any primary or other election for President or Vice President, for electors for President or Vice President, or for Senator or Representative in Congress, shall not be denied or abridged by the United States or any State by reason of failure to pay poll tax or other tax.

Section 2

The Congress shall have power to enforce this article by appropriate legislation.

Amendment XXV

Passed by Congress July 6, 1965. Ratified February 10, 1967.

Section 1

In case of the removal of the President from office or of his death or resignation, the Vice President shall become President.

Section 2

Whenever there is a vacancy in the office of the Vice President, the President shall nominate a Vice President who shall take office upon confirmation by a majority vote of both Houses of Congress.

Section 3

Whenever the President transmits to the President pro tempore of the Senate and the Speaker of the House of Representatives his written declaration that he is unable to discharge the powers and duties of his office, and until he transmits to them a written declaration to the contrary, such powers and duties shall be discharged by the Vice President as Acting President.

Section 4

Whenever the Vice President and a majority of either the principal officers of the executive departments or of such other body as Congress may by law provide, transmit to the President pro tempore of the Senate and the Speaker of the House of Representatives their written declaration that the President is unable to discharge the powers and duties of his office, the Vice President shall immediately assume the powers and duties of the office as Acting President.

Thereafter, when the President transmits to the President pro tempore of the Senate and the Speaker of the House of Representatives his written declaration that no inability exists, he shall resume the powers and duties of his office unless the Vice President and a majority of either the principal officers of the executive department or of such other body as Congress may by law provide, transmit within four days to the President pro tempore of the Senate and the Speaker of the House of Representatives their written declaration that the President is unable to discharge the powers and duties of his office. Thereupon Congress shall decide the issue, assembling within forty-eight hours for that purpose if not in session. If the Congress, within twenty-one days after receipt of the latter written declaration, or, if Congress is not in session, within twenty-one days after Congress is required to assemble, determines by two-thirds vote of both Houses that the President is unable to discharge the powers and duties of his office, the Vice President shall continue to discharge the same as Acting President; otherwise, the President shall resume the powers and duties of his office.

Amendment XXVI

Passed by Congress March 23, 1971. Ratified July 1, 1971.

Section 1

The right of citizens of the United States, who are eighteen years of age or older, to vote shall not be denied or abridged by the United States or by any State on account of age.

Section 2

The Congress shall have power to enforce this article by appropriate legislation.

Amendment XXVII

Originally proposed Sept. 25, 1789. Ratified May 7, 1992.

No law, varying the compensation for the services of the Senators and Representatives, shall take effect, until an election of representatives shall have intervened.

★ ★ ★

Concurring Opinion of Justice Clarence Thomas in *United States v. Lopez*

Since the New Deal era, America's steady drift away from constitutionally limited government has been enabled by the Supreme Court's expansive interpretation of the Commerce Clause. Justice Thomas accurately described that judicial revolution in his concurring opinion in United States v. Lopez *(1995).*

In Lopez, the Supreme Court held that Congress lacks authority under the Commerce Clause to criminalize the possession of a firearm in a school zone. The majority opinion, authored by Chief Justice William Rehnquist, concluded in essence that, because firearm possession in a school zone is non-economic activity that has, at best, an attenuated connection to interstate commerce, it is not subject to Congress's Commerce Clause authority.

Justice Thomas agreed that the law was unconstitutional, but authored a separate opinion explaining that the Supreme Court's post-New Deal era interpretation of the Commerce Clause gives Congress nearly limitless power. In addition to creating a constitutional framework that would be utterly foreign to the Founding Fathers, Justice Thomas explained, the Supreme Court's reading of the Commerce Clause is so broad as to suggest that Congress is free to enact laws governing almost every aspect of human existence.

★ ★ ★

UNITED STATES, PETITIONER v. ALFONSO LOPEZ, Jr.
on writ of certiorari to the united states
court of appeals for the fifth circuit
[April 26, 1995]
Justice Thomas, concurring.

The Court today properly concludes that the Commerce Clause does not grant Congress the authority to prohibit gun possession within 1,000 feet of a school, as it attempted to do in the Gun Free School Zones Act of 1990, Pub. L. 101-647, 104 Stat. 4844. Although I join the majority, I write separately to observe that our case law has drifted far from the original understanding of the Commerce Clause. In a future case, we ought to temper our Commerce Clause jurisprudence in a manner that both makes sense of our more recent case law and is more faithful to the original understanding of that Clause.

We have said that Congress may regulate not only "Commerce ... among the several states," U. S. Const., Art. I, §8, cl. 3, but also anything that has a "substantial effect" on such commerce. This test, if taken to its logical extreme, would give Congress a "police power" over all aspects of American life. Unfortunately, we have never come to grips with this implication of our substantial effects formula. Although we have supposedly applied the substantial effects test for the past 60 years, we always have rejected readings of the Commerce Clause and the scope of federal power that would permit Congress to exercise a police power; our cases are quite clear that there are real limits to federal power. See *New York v. United States*, 505 U. S. 144, 155 (1992) ("[N]o one disputes the proposition that '[t]he Constitution created a Federal Government of limited powers'") (quoting *Gregory v. Ashcroft*, 501 U.S. 452, 457 (1991); *Maryland v. Wirtz*, 392 U.S. 183, 196 (1968); *NLRB v. Jones & Laughlin Steel Corp.*, 301 U.S. 1, 37 (1937). Cf. *Chisholm v. Georgia*, 2 Dall. 419, 435 (1793) (Iredell, J.) ("Each State in the Union is sovereign as to all the powers reserved. It must necessarily be so, because the United States have no claim to any authority but such as the States have surrendered to them"). Indeed, on this crucial point, the majority and Justice Breyer agree in principle: the Federal Government has nothing approaching a police power. *Compare ante*, at 7-9 *with post*, at 10-11.

While the principal dissent concedes that there are limits to federal power, the sweeping nature of our current test enables the dissent to argue that Congress can regulate gun possession. But it seems to me that the power to regulate "commerce" can by no means encompass authority over mere gun possession, any more than it empowers the Federal Government to regulate marriage, littering, or cruelty to animals, throughout the 50 States. Our Constitution quite properly leaves such matters to the individual States, notwithstanding these activities' effects on interstate commerce. Any interpretation of the Commerce Clause that even suggests that Congress could regulate such matters is in need of reexamination.

In an appropriate case, I believe that we must further reconsider our "substantial effects" test with an eye toward constructing a standard that reflects the text and history of the Commerce Clause without totally rejecting our more recent Commerce Clause jurisprudence.

Today, however, I merely support the Court's conclusion with a discussion of the text, structure, and history of the Commerce Clause and an analysis of our early case law. My goal is simply to show how far we have departed from the original understanding and to demonstrate that the result we reach today is by no means "radical," *see post*, at 1 (Stevens, J., dissenting). I also want to point out the necessity of refashioning a coherent test that does not tend to "obliterate the distinction between what is national and what is local and create a completely centralized government." *Jones & Laughlin Steel Corp, supra*, at 37.

I

At the time the original Constitution was ratified, "commerce" consisted of selling, buying, and bartering, as well as transporting for these purposes. *See* 1 S. Johnson, A Dictionary of the English Language 361 (4th ed. 1773) (defining commerce as "Intercour[s]e; exchange of one thing for another; interchange of any thing; trade; traffick"); N. Bailey, An Universal Etymological English Dictionary (26th ed. 1789) ("trade or traffic"); T. Sheridan, A Complete Dictionary of the English Language (6th ed. 1796) ("Exchange of one thing for another; trade, traffick"). This understanding finds support in the etymology of the word, which literally means "with merchandise." *See* 3 Oxford English Dictionary 552 (2d ed. 1989) (com—"with"; merci—"merchandise"). In fact, when Federalists and Anti Federalists discussed the Commerce Clause during the ratification period, they often used trade (in its selling/bartering sense) and commerce interchangeably. *See* The Federalist No. 4, p. 22 (J. Jay) (asserting that countries will cultivate our friendship when our "trade" is prudently regulated by Federal Government); [n.1] *id.*, No. 7, at 39-40 (A. Hamilton) (discussing "competitions of commerce" between States resulting from state "regulations of trade"); *id.*, No. 40, at 262 (J. Madison) (asserting that it was an "acknowledged object of the Convention ... that the regulation of trade should be submitted to the general government"); Lee, Letters of a Federal Farmer No. 5, in Pamphlets on the Constitution of the United States 319 (P. Ford ed. 1888); Smith, An Address to the People of the State of New York, in *id.*, at 107.

As one would expect, the term "commerce" was used in contradistinction to productive activities such as manufacturing and agriculture. Alexander Hamilton, for example, repeatedly treated commerce, agriculture, and manufacturing as three separate endeavors. See, e.g., The Federalist No. 36, at 224 (referring to "agriculture, commerce, manufactures"); *id.*, No. 21, at 133 (distinguishing commerce, arts, and industry); *id.*, No. 12, at 74 (asserting that commerce and agriculture have shared interests). The same distinctions were made in the state ratification conventions. *See e.g.*, 2 Debates in the Several State Conventions on the Adoption of the Federal Constitution 57 (J. Elliot ed. 1836) (hereinafter Debates) (T. Dawes at Massachusetts convention); *id.*, at 336 (M. Smith at New York convention).

Moreover, interjecting a modern sense of commerce into the Constitution generates significant textual and structural problems. For example, one cannot replace "commerce" with a different type of enterprise, such as manufacturing. When a manufacturer produces a car, assembly cannot take place "with a foreign nation" or "with the Indian Tribes." Parts may come from different States or other nations and hence may have been in the flow of commerce at one time, but manufacturing takes place at a discrete site. Agriculture and manufacturing involve the production of goods; commerce encompasses traffic in such articles.

The Port Preference Clause also suggests that the term "commerce" denoted sale and/or transport rather than business generally. According to that Clause, "[n]o Preference shall be given by any Regulation of Commerce or Revenue to the Ports of one State over those of another." U. S. Const., Art. I, §9, cl. 6. Although it is possible to conceive of regulations of manufacturing or farming that prefer one port over another, the more natural reading is that the Clause prohibits Congress from using its commerce power to channel commerce through certain favored ports.

The Constitution not only uses the word "commerce" in a narrower sense than our case law might suggest, it also does not support the proposition that Congress has authority over all activities that "substantially affect" interstate commerce. The Commerce Clause [n.2] does not state that Congress may "regulate matters that substantially affect commerce with foreign Nations, and among the several States, and with the Indian Tribes." In contrast, the Constitution itself temporarily prohibited amendments that would "affect" Congress' lack of authority to prohibit or restrict the slave trade or to enact unproportioned direct taxation. U. S. Const., Art. V. Clearly, the Framers could have drafted a Constitution that contained a "substantially affects interstate commerce" clause had that been their objective.

In addition to its powers under the Commerce Clause, Congress has the authority to enact such laws as are "necessary and proper" to carry into execution its power to regulate commerce among the several States. U. S. Const., Art. I, §8, cl. 18. But on this Court's understanding of congressional power under these two Clauses, many of Congress' other enumerated powers under Art. I, §8 are wholly superfluous. After all, if Congress may regulate all matters that substantially affect commerce, there is no need for the Constitution to specify that Congress may enact bankruptcy laws, cl. 4, or coin money and fix the standard of weights and measures, cl. 5, or punish counterfeiters of United States coin and securities, cl. 6. Likewise, Congress would not need the separate authority to establish post-offices and post-roads, cl. 7, or to grant patents and copyrights, cl. 8, or to "punish Piracies and Felonies committed on the high Seas," cl. 10. It might not even need the power to raise and support an Army and Navy, cls. 12 and 13, for fewer people would engage in commercial shipping if they thought that a foreign power could expropriate their property with ease. Indeed, if Congress could regulate matters that substantially affect interstate commerce, there would have been no need to specify that Congress can regulate international trade and commerce with the Indians. As the Framers surely understood, these other branches of trade substantially affect interstate commerce.

Put simply, much if not all of Art. I, §8 (including portions of the Commerce Clause itself) would be surplusage if Congress had been given authority over matters that substantially affect interstate commerce. An interpretation of cl. 3 that makes the rest of §8 superfluous simply cannot be correct. Yet this Court's Commerce Clause jurisprudence has endorsed just such an interpretation: the power we have accorded Congress has swallowed Art. I, §8. [n.3]

Indeed, if a "substantial effects" test can be appended to the Commerce Clause, why not to every other power of the Federal Government? There is no reason for singling out the Commerce Clause for special treatment. Accordingly, Congress could regulate all matters that "substantially affect" the Army and Navy, bankruptcies, tax collection, expenditures, and so on. In that case, the clauses of §8 all mutually overlap, something we can assume the Founding Fathers never intended.

II

Our construction of the scope of congressional authority has the additional problem of coming close to turning the Tenth Amendment on its head. Our case law could be read to reserve to the United States all powers not expressly prohibited by the Constitution. Taken together, these fundamental textual problems should, at the very least, convince us that the "substantial effects" test should be reexamined.

The exchanges during the ratification campaign reveal the relatively limited reach of the Commerce Clause and of federal power generally. The Founding Fathers confirmed that most areas of life (even many matters that would have substantial effects on commerce) would remain outside the reach of the Federal Government. Such affairs would continue to be under the exclusive control of the States.

Early Americans understood that commerce, manufacturing, and agriculture, while distinct activities, were intimately related and dependent on each other—that each "substantially affected" the others. After all, items produced by farmers and manufacturers were the primary articles of commerce at the time. If commerce was more robust as a result of federal superintendence, farmers and manufacturers could benefit. Thus, Oliver Ellsworth of Connecticut attempted to convince farmers of the benefits of regulating commerce. "Your property and riches depend on a

ready demand and generous price for the produce you can annually spare," he wrote, and these conditions exist "where trade
flourishes and when the merchant can freely export the produce
of the country" to nations that will pay the highest price. A
Landholder No. 1, Connecticut Courant, Nov. 5, 1787, in 3
Documentary History of the Ratification of the Constitution 399
(M. Jensen ed. 1978) (hereinafter Documentary History). See
also The Federalist No. 35, at 219 (A. Hamilton)
("[D]iscerning citizens are well aware that the mechanic and
manufacturing arts furnish the materials of mercantile enterprise
and industry. Many of them indeed are immediately connected
with the operations of commerce. They know that the merchant
is their natural patron and friend"); id., at 221 ("Will not the
merchant ... be disposed to cultivate ... the interests of the
mechanic and manufacturing arts to which his commerce is so
nearly allied?"); A Jerseyman: To the Citizens of New Jersey,
Trenton Mercury, Nov. 6, 1787, in 3 Documentary History 147
(noting that agriculture will serve as a "source of commerce");
Marcus, The New Jersey Journal, Nov. 14, 1787, id., at 152
(both the mechanic and the farmer benefit from the prosperity
of commerce). William Davie, a delegate to the North Carolina
Convention, illustrated the close link best:

> Commerce, sir, is the nurse of [agriculture and manu
> facturing]. The merchant furnishes the planter with
> such articles as he cannot manufacture himself, and
> finds him a market for his produce. Agriculture can
> not flourish if commerce languishes; they are mutu
> ally dependent on each other.

4 Debates 20. Yet, despite being well aware that agriculture, manufacturing, and other matters substantially affected commerce, the founding generation did not cede authority over all these activities to Congress. Hamilton, for instance, acknowledged that the Federal Government could not regulate agriculture and like concerns:

> The administration of private justice between the citizens of the same State, the supervision of agriculture and of other concerns of a similar nature, all those things in short which are proper to be provided for by local legislation, can never be desirable cares of a general jurisdiction.

The Federalist No. 17, at 106. In the unlikely event that the Federal Government would attempt to exercise authority over such matters, its effort "would be as troublesome as it would be nugatory." *Ibid.* [n.4]

The comments of Hamilton and others about federal power reflected the well known truth that the new Government would have only the limited and enumerated powers found in the Constitution. *See, e.g.,* 2 Debates 267-268 (A. Hamilton at New York convention) (noting that there would be just cause for rejecting the Constitution if it would enable the Federal Government to "alter, or abrogate ... [a state's] civil and criminal institutions [or] penetrate the recesses of domestic life, and control, in all respects, the private conduct of individuals"); The Federalist No. 45, at 313 (J. Madison); 3 Debates 259 (J. Madison) (Virginia convention); R. Sherman & O. Ellsworth, Letter to Governor Huntington, Sept.

26, 1787, in 3 Documentary History 352; J. Wilson, Speech in the State House Yard, Oct. 6, 1787, in 2 *id.*, at 167-168. Agriculture and manufacture, since they were not surrendered to the Federal Government, were state concerns. See The Federalist No. 34, at 212-213 (A. Hamilton) (observing that the "internal encouragement of agriculture and manufactures" was an object of state expenditure). Even before the passage of the Tenth Amendment, it was apparent that Congress would possess only those powers "herein granted" by the rest of the Constitution. U. S. Const., Art. I, §1.

Where the Constitution was meant to grant federal authority over an activity substantially affecting interstate commerce, the Constitution contains an enumerated power over that particular activity. Indeed, the Framers knew that many of the other enumerated powers in §8 dealt with matters that substantially affected interstate commerce. Madison, for instance, spoke of the bankruptcy power as being "intimately connected with the regulation of commerce." The Federalist No. 42, at 287. Likewise, Hamilton urged that "[i]f we mean to be a commercial people or even to be secure on our Atlantic side, we must endeavour as soon as possible to have a navy." *Id.*, No. 24, at 157 (A. Hamilton).

In short, the Founding Fathers were well aware of what the principal dissent calls "'economic ... realities.'" *See post*, at 11-12 (Breyer, J.) (citing North American Co. v. SEC, 327 U.S. 686, 705 (1946)). Even though the boundary between commerce and other matters may ignore "economic reality" and thus seem arbitrary or artificial to some, we must nevertheless respect a constitutional line that does not grant Congress power over all that substantially affects interstate commerce.

III

If the principal dissent's understanding of our early case law were correct, there might be some reason to doubt this view of the original understanding of the Constitution. According to that dissent, Chief Justice Marshall's opinion in *Gibbons v. Ogden*, 9 Wheat. 1 (1824) established that Congress may control all local activities that "significantly affect interstate commerce," *post*, at 1. And, "with the exception of one wrong turn subsequently corrected," this has been the "traditiona[l]" method of interpreting the Commerce Clause. *Post*, at 18 (citing *Gibbons* and *United States v. Darby*, 312 U.S. 100, 116-117 (1941)).

In my view, the dissent is wrong about the holding and reasoning of Gibbons. Because this error leads the dissent to characterize the first 150 years of this Court's case law as a "wrong turn," I feel compelled to put the last 50 years in proper perspective.

A

In Gibbons, the Court examined whether a federal law that licensed ships to engage in the "coasting trade" pre-empted a New York law granting a 30 year monopoly to Robert Livingston and Robert Fulton to navigate the State's waterways by steamship. In concluding that it did, the Court noted that Congress could regulate "navigation" because

> [a]ll America ... has uniformly understood, the word 'commerce,' to comprehend navigation. It was so understood, and must have been so understood, when the constitution was framed. *9 Wheat., at 190.*

The Court also observed that federal power over commerce "among the several States" meant that Congress could regulate commerce conducted partly within a State. Because a portion of interstate commerce and foreign commerce would almost always take place within one or more States, federal power over interstate and foreign commerce necessarily would extend into the States. *Id.*, at 194-196.

At the same time, the Court took great pains to make clear that Congress could not regulate commerce "which is completely internal, which is carried on between man and man in a State, or between different parts of the same State, and which does not extend to or affect other States." Id., at 194. Moreover, while suggesting that the Constitution might not permit States to regulate interstate or foreign commerce, the Court observed that "[i]nspection laws, quarantine laws, health laws of every description, as well as laws for regulating the internal commerce of a State" were but a small part "of that immense mass of legislation ... not surrendered to a general government." *Id.*, at 203. From an early moment, the Court rejected the notion that Congress can regulate everything that affects interstate commerce. That the internal commerce of the States and the numerous state inspection, quarantine, and health laws had substantial effects on interstate commerce cannot be doubted. Nevertheless, they were not "surrendered to the general government."

Of course, the principal dissent is not the first to misconstrue *Gibbons*. For instance, the Court has stated that *Gibbons* "described the federal commerce power with a breadth never yet exceeded." *Wickard v. Filburn*, 317 U.S. 111, 120 (1942). See also *Perez v. United States*, 402 U.S. 146, 151 (1971) (claiming that with *Darby* and *Wickard*, "the broader view of the Commerce Clause announced by Chief Justice Marshall had been restored"). I believe that this misreading stems from two statements in *Gibbons*.

First, the Court made the uncontroversial claim that federal power does not encompass *"commerce"* that "does not extend to or affect other States." 9 Wheat., at 194 (emphasis added). From this statement, the principal dissent infers that whenever an activity affects interstate commerce, it necessarily follows that Congress can regulate such activities. Of course, Chief Justice Marshall said no such thing and the inference the dissent makes cannot be drawn.

There is a much better interpretation of the "affect[s]" language: because the Court had earlier noted that the commerce power did not extend to wholly intrastate commerce, the Court was acknowledging that although the line between intrastate and interstate/foreign commerce would be difficult to draw, federal authority could not be construed to cover purely intrastate commerce. Commerce that did not affect another State could *never* be said to be commerce "among the several States."

But even if one were to adopt the dissent's reading, the "affect[s]" language, at most, permits Congress to regulate only intrastate commerce that substantially affects interstate and foreign commerce. There is no reason to believe that Chief Justice Marshall was asserting that Congress could regulate all activities that affect interstate commerce. *See Ibid.*

The second source of confusion stems from the Court's praise for the Constitution's division of power between the States and the Federal Government:

> The genius and character of the whole government seem to be, that its action is to be applied to all the external concerns of the nation, and to those internal concerns which affect the States generally; but not to those which are completely within a particular State, which do not affect other States, and with which it is not necessary to interfere, for the purpose of executing some of the general powers of the government.

Id., at 195. In this passage, the Court merely was making the well understood point that the Constitution commits matters of "national" concern to Congress and leaves "local" matters to the States. The Court was *not* saying that whatever Congress believes is a national matter becomes an object of federal control. The matters of national concern are enumerated in the Constitution: war, taxes, patents, and copyrights, uniform rules of naturalization and bankruptcy, types of commerce, and so on. *See generally* U. S. Const., Art. I, §8. *Gibbons'* emphatic statements that Congress could not regulate many matters that affect commerce confirm that the Court did not read the Commerce Clause as granting Congress control over matters that "affect the States generally." [n.5] *Gibbons* simply cannot be construed as the principal dissent would have it.

B

I am aware of no cases prior to the New Deal that characterized the power flowing from the Commerce Clause as sweepingly as does our substantial effects test. My review of the case law indicates that the substantial effects test is but an innovation of the 20th century.

Even before *Gibbons*, Chief Justice Marshall, writing for the Court in *Cohens v. Virginia*, 6 Wheat. 264 (1821), noted that Congress had "no general right to punish murder committed within any of the States," *id.*, at 426, and that it was "clear that congress cannot punish felonies generally," *id.*, at 428. The Court's only qualification was that Congress could enact such laws for places where it enjoyed plenary powers—for instance, over the District of Columbia. *Id.*, at 426. Thus, whatever effect ordinary murders, or robbery, or gun possession might have on interstate commerce (or on any other subject of federal concern) was irrelevant to the question of congressional power. [n.6]

United States v. Dewitt, 9 Wall. 41 (1870), marked the first time the Court struck down a federal law as exceeding the power conveyed by the Commerce Clause. In a two-page opinion, the Court invalidated a nationwide law prohibiting all sales of naphtha and illuminating oils. In so doing, the Court remarked that the Commerce Clause

> has always been understood as limited by its terms; and as a virtual denial of any power to interfere with the internal trade and business of the separate States.

Id., at 44. The law in question was "plainly a regulation of police," which could have constitutional application only where Congress had exclusive authority, such as the territories. *Id.*, at 44-45. *See also License Tax Cases*, 5 Wall. 462, 470-471 (1867) (Congress cannot interfere with the internal commerce and business of a State); *Trade-Mark Cases*, 100 U.S. 82 (1879) (Congress cannot regulate internal commerce and thus may not establish national trademark registration).

In *United States v. E. C. Knight Co.*, 156 U.S. 1 (1895), this Court held that mere attempts to monopolize the manufacture of sugar could not be regulated pursuant to the Commerce Clause. Raising echoes of the discussions of the Framers regarding the intimate relationship between commerce and manufacturing, the Court declared that "[c]ommerce succeeds to manufacture, and is not a part of it." *Id.*, at 12. The Court also approvingly quoted from *Kidd v. Pearson*, 128 U.S. 1, 20 (1888):

> "'No distinction is more popular to the common mind, or more clearly expressed in economic and political literature, than that between manufacture and commerce.... If it be held that the term [commerce] includes the regulation of all such manufactures as are intended to be the subject of commercial transactions in the future, it is impossible to deny that it would also include all productive industries that contemplate the same thing. The result would be that Congress would be invested ... with the power to regulate, not only manufactures, but also agriculture, horticulture, stock raising, domestic fisheries, mining—in short, every branch of human industry.'"

E. C. Knight, 156 U. S., at 14. If federal power extended to these types of production "comparatively little of business operations and affairs would be left for state control." *Id.*, at 16. See also *Newberry v. United States*, 256 U.S. 232, 257 (1921) ("It is settled ... that the power to regulate interstate and foreign commerce does not reach whatever is essential thereto. Without agriculture, manufacturing, mining, etc., commerce could not exist, but this fact does not suffice to subject them to the control of Congress"). Whether or not manufacturing, agriculture, or other matters substantially affected interstate commerce was irrelevant.

As recently as 1936, the Court continued to insist that the Commerce Clause did not reach the wholly internal business of the States. See *Carter v. Carter Coal Co.*, 298 U.S. 238, 308 (1936) (Congress may not regulate mine labor because "[t]he relation of employer and employee is a local relation"); see also *A. L. A. Schechter Poultry Corp. v. United States*, 295 U.S. 495, 543-550 (1935) (holding that Congress may not regulate intrastate sales of sick chickens or the labor of employees involved in intrastate poultry sales). The Federal Government simply could not reach such subjects regardless of their effects on interstate commerce.

These cases all establish a simple point: from the time of the ratification of the Constitution to the mid 1930's, it was widely understood that the Constitution granted Congress only limited powers, notwithstanding the Commerce Clause. [n.7] Moreover, there was no question that activities wholly separated from business, such as gun possession, were beyond the reach of the commerce power. If anything, the "wrong turn" was the Court's dramatic departure in the 1930's from a century and a half of precedent.

IV

Apart from its recent vintage and its corresponding lack of any grounding in the original understanding of the Constitution, the substantial effects test suffers from the further flaw that it appears to grant Congress a police power over the Nation. When asked at oral argument if there were *any* limits to the Commerce Clause, the Government was at a loss for words. Tr. of Oral Arg. 5. Likewise, the principal dissent insists that there are limits, but it cannot muster even one example. *Post*, at 10-11. Indeed, the dissent implicitly concedes that its reading has no limits when it criticizes the Court for "threaten[ing] legal uncertainty in an area of law that ... seemed reasonably well settled." *Post*, at 17-18. The one advantage of the dissent's standard is certainty: it is certain that under its analysis everything may be regulated under the guise of the Commerce Clause.

The substantial effects test suffers from this flaw, in part, because of its "aggregation principle." Under so called "class of activities" statutes, Congress can regulate whole categories of activities that are not themselves either "interstate" or "commerce." In applying the effects test, we ask whether the class of activities as a whole substantially affects interstate commerce, not whether any specific activity within the class has such effects when considered in isolation. See *Maryland v. Wirtz*, 392 U. S., at 192-193 (if class of activities is "'within the reach of federal power,'" courts may not excise individual applications as trivial) (quoting *Darby*, 312 U. S., at 120-121).

The aggregation principle is clever, but has no stopping point. Suppose all would agree that gun possession within 1,000 feet of a school does not substantially affect commerce, but that possession of weapons generally (knives, brass knuckles, nunchakus, etc.) does. Under our substantial effects doctrine, even though Congress cannot single out gun possession, it can prohibit weapon possession generally. But one always can draw the circle broadly enough to cover an activity that, when taken in isolation, would not have substantial effects on commerce. Under our jurisprudence, if Congress passed an omnibus "substantially affects interstate commerce" statute, purporting to regulate every aspect of human existence, the Act apparently would be constitutional. Even though particular sections may govern only trivial activities, the statute in the aggregate regulates matters that substantially affect commerce.

V

This extended discussion of the original understanding and our first century and a half of case law does not necessarily require a wholesale abandonment of our more recent opinions. [n.8] It simply reveals that our substantial effects test is far removed from both the Constitution and from our early case law and that the Court's opinion should not be viewed as "radical" or another "wrong turn" that must be corrected in the future. [n.9] The analysis also suggests that we ought to temper our Commerce Clause jurisprudence.

Unless the dissenting Justices are willing to repudiate our long held understanding of the limited nature of federal power, I would think that they too must be willing to reconsider the substantial effects test in a future case. If we wish to be true to a Constitution that does not cede a police power to the Federal Government, our Commerce Clause's boundaries simply cannot be "defined" as being "'commensurate with the national needs'" or self consciously intended to let the Federal Government "'defend itself against economic forces that Congress decrees inimical or destructive of the national economy.'" *See post*, at 12-13 (Breyer, J., dissenting) (quoting *North American Co. v. SEC*, 327 U.S. 686, 705 (1946)). Such a formulation of federal power is no test at all: it is a blank check.

At an appropriate juncture, I think we must modify our Commerce Clause jurisprudence. Today, it is easy enough to say that the Clause certainly does not empower Congress to ban gun possession within 1,000 feet of a school.

Notes

1. All references to The Federalist are to the Jacob E. Cooke 1961 edition.

2. Even to speak of "the Commerce Clause" perhaps obscures the actual scope of that Clause. As an original matter, Congress did not have authority to regulate all commerce; Congress could only "regulate Commerce with foreign Nations, and among the several States, and with the Indian Tribes." U. S. Const., Art. I, §8, cl. 3. Although the precise line between interstate/foreign commerce and purely intrastate commerce was hard to draw, the Court attempted to adhere to such a line for the first 150 years of our Nation. See infra, at 593–599.

3. There are other powers granted to Congress outside of Art. I, §8 that may become wholly superfluous as well due to our distortion of the Commerce Clause. For instance, Congress has plenary power over the District of Columbia and the territories. See U. S. Const., Art. I, §8, cl. 15 and Art. IV, §3, cl. 2. The grant of comprehensive legislative power over certain areas of the Nation, when

read in conjunction with the rest of the Constitution, further confirms that Congress was not ceded plenary authority over the whole Nation.

4. Cf. 3 Debates 40 (E. Pendleton at the Virginia convention) (the proposed Federal Government "does not intermeddle with the local, particular affairs of the states. Can Congress legislate for the state of Virginia? Can [it] make a law altering the form of transferring property, or the rule of descents, in Virginia?"); id., at 553 (J. Marshall at the Virginia convention) (denying that Congress could make "laws affecting the mode of transferring property, or contracts, or claims, between citizens of the same state"); The Federalist No. 33, at 206 (A. Hamilton) (denying that Congress could change laws of descent or could pre-empt a land tax); A Native of Virginia: Observations upon the Proposed Plan of Federal Government, Apr. 2, 1788, in 9 Documentary History 692 (States have sole authority over "rules of property").

5. None of the other Commerce Clause opinions during Chief Justice Marshall's tenure, which concerned the "dormant" Commerce Clause, even suggested that Congress had authority over all matters substantially affecting commerce. See Brown v. Maryland, 12 Wheat. 419 (1827); Willson v. Black Bird Creek Marsh Co., 2 Pet. 245 (1829).

6. It is worth noting that Congress, in the first federal criminal Act, did not establish nationwide prohibitions against murder and the like. See Act of April 30, 1790, ch. 9, 1 Stat. 112. To be sure, Congress outlawed murder, manslaughter, maiming, and larceny, but only when those acts were either committed on United States territory not part of a State or on the high seas.

Ibid. See U. S. Const., Art. I, §8, cl. 10 (authorizing Congress to outlaw piracy and felonies on high seas); Art. IV, §3, cl. 2 (plenary authority over United States territory and property). When Congress did enact nationwide criminal laws, it acted pursuant to direct grants of authority found in the Constitution. Compare Act of April 30, 1790, supra, §§1 and 14 (prohibitions against treason and the counterfeiting of U. S. securities) with U. S. Const., Art. I, §8, cl. 6 (counterfeiting); Art. III, §3, cl. 2 (treason). Notwithstanding any substantial effects that murder, kidnaping, or gun possession might have had on interstate commerce, Congress understood that it could not establish nationwide prohibitions.

Likewise, there were no laws in the early Congresses that regulated manufacturing and agriculture. Nor was there any statute which purported to regulate activities with "substantial effects" on interstate commerce.

7.   To be sure, congressional power pursuant to the Commerce Clause was alternatively described less narrowly or more narrowly during this 150 year period. Compare United States v. Coombs, 12 Pet. 72, 78 (1838) (commerce power "extends to such acts, done on land, which interfere with, obstruct, or prevent the due exercise of the power to regulate [interstate and international] commerce" such as stealing goods from a beached ship) with United States v. E. C. Knight Co., 156 U.S. 1, 13 (1895) ("Contracts to buy, sell, or exchange goods to be transported among the several States, the transportation and its instrumentalities ... may be regulated, but this is because they form part of interstate trade or commerce"). During this period, however, this Court never held that Congress could regulate everything that substantially affects commerce.

8. Although I might be willing to return to the original understanding, I recognize that many believe that it is too late in the day to undertake a fundamental reexamination of the past 60 years. Consideration of stare decisis and reliance interests may convince us that we cannot wipe the slate clean.

9. Nor can the majority's opinion fairly be compared to Lochner v. New York, 198 U.S. 45 (1905). See post, at 1-7 (Souter, J., dissenting). Unlike Lochner and our more recent "substantive due process" cases, today's decision enforces only the Constitution and not "judicial policy judgments." See post, at 5. Notwithstanding Justice Souter's discussion, "'commercial character'" is not only a natural but an inevitable "ground of Commerce Clause distinction." See post, at 6 (emphasis added). Our invalidation of the Gun Free School Zones Act therefore falls comfortably within our proper role in reviewing federal legislation to determine if it exceeds congressional authority as defined by the Constitution itself. As John Marshall put it:

> If [Congress] were to make a law not warranted by any of the powers enumerated, it would be considered by the judges as an infringement of the Constitution which they are to guard.... They would declare it void.

3 Debates 553 (before the Virginia ratifying convention); see also The Federalist No. 44, at 305 (James Madison) (asserting that if Congress exercises powers "not warranted by [the Constitution's] true meaning" the judiciary will defend the Constitution); id., No. 78, at 526 (A. Hamilton) (asserting that the "courts of justice are to be considered as the bulwarks of a limited constitu-

tion against legislative encroachments"). Where, as here, there is a case or controversy, there can be no "misstep", post, at 13, in enforcing the Constitution.

Acknowledgments

I am grateful to all who encouraged me to write this book and assisted in its preparation and publication, including Jeff Carneal, Jack Langer, Boyd Matheson, Marji Ross, Chip Roy, and Robert Stander. I am especially grateful to my wife Sharon, who inspires and assists me in all things and contributed substantially to the contents of this book.

Notes

Introduction

1. "Text of President Obama's State of the Union Address," *Washington Post,* January 26, 2011, http://www.washingtonpost.com/wp-dyn/content/article/2011/01/25/AR2011012506398.html (accessed May 25, 2011).

2. "N.J. to receive $913M more in tax revenue than expected," *The Star-Ledger,* May 17, 2011; and "N.J. treasurer predicts state's revenue bump will be smaller than projected $913M," *The Star-Ledger,* May 17, 2011.

Chapter 2

1. A letter of marque and reprisal is a "hall pass" of sorts that
    entitles its holder to engage in state-sponsored acts of piracy on
    the high seas in the name of the United States. Although these
    letters are generally considered obsolete and are rarely discussed
    these days, it has long been a dream of mine to receive this kind
    of sanction and fulfill my childhood dream of being a pirate
    without committing a crime.

Chapter 5

1. Remember, currently every dollar of the revenue the federal gov-
    ernment collects each year—about $2.2 trillion annually—is
    spent on entitlements and interest on the national debt, such that
    funding for defense and every other government function must
    be secured entirely through borrowing. We are borrowing roughly
    $1.65 trillion per year, about 43 percent of annual federal outlays,
    just to pay for national defense and the basic operations of gov-
    ernment.

2. Congress could minimize this and other problems associated with
    the debt ceiling by enacting legislation that instructs the executive
    branch on how to spend federal revenue during a debt-ceiling-
    induced shortfall. That legislation could provide, for example,
    that during such a shortfall the first money in the door each
    month must be used to pay interest on national debt, Social
    Security benefits, and the salaries of active-duty military person-
    nel. In that scenario, the president's discretion would extend only
    to funds remaining after the specified payments had been made

    Another option would be for Congress to pass legislation
    providing that, unless or until Congress adopts a new budget,
    raises the debt ceiling, or otherwise resolves a debt-ceiling-induced
    shortfall, all expenditures aside from interest on the debt must be
    discounted at a rate reflecting the would-be annual deficit. In

other words, if X percent of the current federal budget could be funded only through deficit spending, the entire budget and each item therein (aside from interest payments) would be discounted by X percent.

Neither of these options would eliminate the pain and uncertainty associated with a debt-ceiling-induced shortfall, nor would either option be acceptable except on a long-term basis. Nevertheless, both approaches (especially the second) would give Congress a middle-ground alternative to the Hobson's choice it tends to face each time it hits the debt ceiling: either (a) raise the debt ceiling, thereby perpetuating a problem that the American people know could cripple our entire economy, or (b) don't raise the debt ceiling, risk the onset of economic and political chaos, and implicitly grant the president unprecedented power over federal spending.

3. No matter how unfair this might seem, we must remember that in a free society with a robust economy, every able-bodied, sound-minded citizen has a chance to become wealthy.

4. "Poll: Large majority support balanced budget amendment to Constitution," *The Daily Caller*, May 27, 2011, http://dailycaller. com/2011/05/27/poll-large-majority-support-balanced-budget-amendment-to-constitution/ (accessed May 31, 2011).

Chapter 6

1. Data available at www.usgovernmentspending.com (accessed June 1, 2011).

2. Ibid.

3. Ibid.

4. See James C. Cooper, "Budget Deficit: Government Handouts Top Tax Income," *The Fiscal Times*, April 18, 2011, http://www. thefiscaltimes.com/Columns/2011/04/18/Budget-Deficit-

Government-Handouts-Top-Tax-Income.aspx (accessed June 1, 2011).

Chapter 7

1.   There is only one branch of government run by people who, once installed, are supposed to be insulated from the political process: the judiciary. Once nominated by the president and confirmed by the Senate, federal judges and justices serve without being subject to the public's political whims. This is with good reason: their job is not to make laws or enforce them, but to interpret them.

If judges and justices were subject to the electoral process, the task of interpreting the law would inevitably slide into the realm of making law (even more than it already does), which would ultimately make lawmakers less accountable to the people they serve. It is therefore because of the need to keep lawmakers accountable to the people, and not in spite of that need, that we insulate judges and justices from the electoral process. The same cannot be said of executive branch officials.

Index

COMING FALL 2011

Regnery Publishing Presents...

REGNERY HISTORY

History is full of heroes and villains, stories and back stories.
But too often, only one side of the story reaches the public.
That's why Regnery Publishing is proud to announce the launch
of its new imprint **Regnery History**! Beginning in fall 2011,
Regnery History will introduce the most fascinating and captivating
titles within the history, biography, and military categories.

Our **Regnery History** titles will offer you:

★ A politically incorrect perspective on the figures
and topics that deserve attention, but may have been
ignored, overlooked, or even covered up in the past

★ Compelling and comprehensive biographies

★ An entertaining and educating journey into our past
that will change the way you see history forever

To learn more, go to

RegneryHistory.com

facebook   twitter